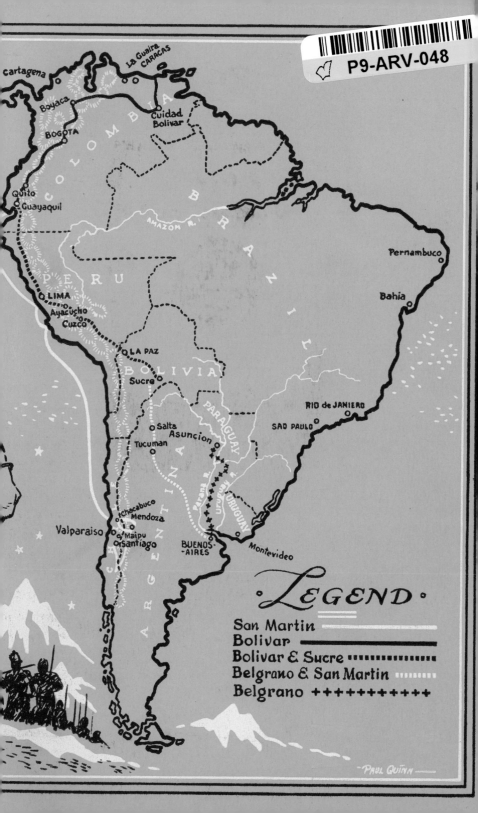

P9-ARV-048

cartagena
La Guaira
CARACAS
Boyaca
Cuidad
Bolivar
BOGOTA
COLOMBIA
BRAZIL
Quito
Guayaquil
AMAZON R.
Pernambuco
P E R U
Bahia
LIMA
Ayacucho
Cuzco
LA PAZ
BOLIVIA
Sucre
RIO de JANIERO
PARAGUAY
SAO PAULO
Salta
Asuncion
Tucuman
ARGENTINA
Chacabuco
Mendoza
Valparaiso
Maipu
Santiago
BUENOS
-AIRES
Montevideo
URUGUAY

· LEGEND ·

San Martin	══════
Bolivar	──────
Bolivar & Sucre	●●●●●●●●●●●
Belgrano & San Martin	░░░░░░░
Belgrano	++++++++++

—PAUL QUINN—

LIBERATORS AND HEROES OF SOUTH AMERICA

LIBERATORS and HEROES of SOUTH AMERICA

☆ ☆ ☆ ☆

by

MARION LANSING

Illustrated by Paul Quinn

L. C. Page & Company
Publishers · Boston

PREFACE

Fifty or one hundred years from now—or perhaps much sooner—the tale of the Americas will doubtless be told as a single story, with the North American chapters fitted in with those of South America. The story of the South American Wars of Independence will follow the account of our American Revolution as part of the triumphant struggle of the New World to free itself from the domination of the Old World.

There will be a joint list of heroes, too, an All-American list, with Simón Bolívar matching George Washington, and other leaders of the early days of the South American republics placed side by side with our own honored men. But if that list were to be made up today, we of the United States would find ourselves all too unfamiliar with the names nominated by our sister republics of the south. Three or four of the outstanding figures would be known by name, but even for them we could not fill in the dramatic background of their lives and achievements. Others who are highly honored in their own countries might be almost, if not quite, unknown to us.

This book is intended to fill in, so far as space allows, South American names for that All-American list. It tells particularly of the group of "liberators," for that period in the "heroic age" of South America. But it includes brief stories of men who placed their stamp on the young republics by their interest in education and progressive government, as well as by their struggles for freedom. They are a picturesque and varied group, these South Americans, who make a distinct contribution to our picture of American backgrounds and traditions at this time when the threads of the pattern of the two continents are being woven together as they have not been for a hundred years. It is interesting to go back to Bolívar's dream of a canal across the Isthmus of Panama and of a council of Pan-American nations meeting on the Isthmus to consider the problems of the New World as set over against those of the Old World. These men dreamed great dreams which have not yet been completely fulfilled.

The method of the book has been to treat each hero separately in order to make the individuals stand out clearly, but to fit all together so that a continued account emerges. It is interesting to note that each nation brings its important figures.

The sources of the material are too many to list. Nor would their inclusion serve any helpful purpose. Contemporary and modern histories and biographies have been consulted, with travel and descriptive books and journals. Such brief biographies as have resulted can be only suggestive, but they will serve their purpose if they rouse our interest and turn us to a wider range of reading concerning these men and their times.   M. L.

Cambridge, Massachusetts
September, 1940.

CONTENTS

CONTENTS

CONTENTS

CONTENTS

—: x :—

CONTENTS

ILLUSTRATIONS

—: xiii :—

ILLUSTRATIONS

BEFORE THE LIBERATORS

WHEN TWO WORLDS MET

*As a single knight in armor went boldly
ashore to seek out a mysterious empire*

ON a sunshiny day some four hundred years ago a
little company of Spaniards, voyaging south from
Panama along the western coast of South America, came
alongside of a sandy strip of seacoast beyond which they
could see a welcoming harbor with a settlement of low
stone and plaster houses.

They were in waters which no white man had ever

sailed before. They had come through perils of shipwreck and starvation such as would have daunted men of less courage and determination. But still they had pressed on. During the last few weeks they had almost despaired, for the shore which they were skirting seemed to have only endless reaches of tropical forests and swampy jungles. But now the look of the coast had changed. High mountains towered in the distance, and here was a beautiful harbor backed by a sandy plain with signs of this village beyond. Already Indians on their reed rafts were coming out from the harbor. Perhaps this was the gateway of that mysterious empire of Peru where dwelt a mighty Indian ruler who ate off golden plates and was robed in garments covered with gold and silver and precious stones.

It was fifteen years since Francisco Pizarro had come to the New World: fifteen years since he had stood with his leader Balboa on a mountaintop in Panama and gazed at the great southern ocean which they were the first Europeans to see. During those long years there had been rich finds to the north. Cortéz and his little army had discovered the rich empire of Mexico and taken possession of its ruler and its chief city. All Spain had rung with the tale of the golden splendor of Montezuma and his court. But no one had yet found the southern kingdom of which the Indian tribes told such fabulous tales.

This was not Pizarro's first trip southward. He had tried twice before and failed to find anything but the usual huts and villages inhabited by hostile tribes who resisted the advance of the white men. But in almost every village they had entered there had been some sign of gold, and always their guides had told them that it came from the Inca empire in the mountains.

Here there was the same hint of gold. The chief who came out promptly to greet the strangers had rich golden ornaments hanging from his ears. But the gifts he brought in the *balsas* (reed boats) which accompanied him were disappointing. Here were only bananas, pineapples, coconuts, and other less familiar tropical fruits and vegetables, and along with them a number of llamas at which the Spaniards looked curiously. Pizarro had seen Balboa's rough sketches of these Peruvian sheep, but this was his first sight of the long-necked animals themselves, the "little camels," as the Spaniards promptly christened them.

The chief came aboard and was greatly interested in the vessel. He had heard, from his neighbors to the north, of these "houses on the water" of the white men. He stayed for dinner and praised the food and wine. When he left, he invited the Spaniards to visit his town of Tumbez, just inland, and Pizarro made him a present of an iron hatchet, which pleased him greatly for he had never seen its like. All this was according to the usual happenings when an explorer entered a not unfriendly native region. There was nothing to make this meeting different except those huge gold ornaments and the tale of the Indian guides that this was indeed the harbor of the town of Tumbez, outpost of the kingdom hidden behind high mountain ranges.

IN THE INCA TOWN

Pizarro did not go ashore himself to investigate, but sent one of his men, Alonzo de Molina, who took with him as companion an African negro of the crew, and gifts of pigs and poultry, which were unknown to most of the aboriginal tribes. The natives of the seashore received him cordially. They tried to rub the black off the skin of the negro, and marveled when they could not do it. The cock crowed, and they clapped their hands gaily, asking what it was saying.

So far the wonder was all on their side. But when Molina came to his host's house, it was all he could do to keep from showing his astonishment. Here were gold and silver plates in common use, and in the temple there were rich ornaments of gold and silver. The buildings, too, were of good workmanship, better than any they had seen elsewhere.

Molina went back to the vessel with an excited tale of the wonders he had seen, and Pizarro doubted his story's truth. Someone else must go ashore, he said, in whose word he could put more trust. This time the messenger must go farther into the settlement and find out more about it. He must question where such gold as they possessed was found, and what lay in the mountains beyond.

For some reason, this seemed to the ship's company a more dangerous errand. When Pizarro chose Pedro de Candia, a Greek, his friends tried to keep him from going. Perhaps they thought that the Indians had seemed friendly because they were taken by surprise. If their temple was

LLAMAS IN PERU
The Spaniards were much interested in these "little camels,"
as they called them.

such a rich and remarkable place of worship, they would have grown fearful in the interval. The visitor might not get back so easily this time. But Candia would not listen to their cautions.

"Determined am I," he said, "to go alone and explore yonder valley. If they slay me, you, my comrades, will have lost little or nothing in me. But if things turn out to my desire, then will our victory be great indeed."

That speech, and the episode that followed, show the spirit with which these men of the sixteenth century went about their business of exploration and conquest. If anything happened to them, it would be in the line of their adventure and must be accepted. But if they succeeded, untold treasures might fall into their hands.

So this Spanish freebooter arrayed himself as he would in his homeland for any knightly adventure. He put on his coat of mail and his steel helmet, belted on his sword, slung his musket over his shoulder, and went ashore alone, carrying for his greater protection a huge wooden cross, symbol of his Christian faith. A single knight sallying forth to investigate what might prove to be the Inca empire!

Is it any wonder that the simple natives marveled at him? This man with the shining coat might be another Child of the Sun, coming to them from the Great Sun Father whom they worshipped, even as their own Inca emperors came to them in times past.

The old record gives every detail of the picture. They welcomed him cordially and examined his strange costume and possessions. Some of them had heard of these queer fire-sticks of the white men. They looked at this one closely and then asked him to "let it speak." Candia set up a wooden target and fired at it, and the people fell on their faces in fright. But when they got timidly up, the stranger was still smiling pleasantly at them. They did not know that their wonder was being matched by his. He was marveling at the great stone temple with carved animals crouched on either side of the doorway and carved emblems on its walls.

The animals were not all of stone. As Candia walked along, a caged jaguar was let loose, whether by accident or with a purpose, who shall say? The creature leaped at him with teeth bared, ready to sink them into his flesh. He lifted his holy cross, and the jaguar fell back. So the story runs. But did the sharp teeth try to bite into the steel coat and fail?

The Spaniard was royally entertained and saw such marvels as had never entered his dreams. Here in the palace were the gold and silver plates of which there had been so many tales, and jeweled hangings and rich carved seats. These were civilized people who lived in comfort and even luxury. There was a woman's house where dwelt the virgins of the temple worship, and next to it was their secret garden with gold and silver copies of fruits and vegetables. He went into the temple workrooms where skilled craftsmen were making these articles.

Candia went back to the ship with his story. Probably he boasted a little and exaggerated more. But the truth was sufficient. This town of Tumbez was only an outpost of the Inca empire, but its rich possessions were accounted for by the fact that it was often visited by the emperors themselves when they returned from victories over the tribes that lived farther to the north. The center of the empire was, he had learned, far up in the mountains in the valley of Cuzco. Here the ruling Inca, Atahualpa, was at this moment dwelling in richness that could not be imagined.

The greatest marvel Candia had to relate was that these natives did not seem to know the value of their gold and silver. They used them because they liked their shining brightness, and because these metals were common and abundant. That was what the Spaniards could hardly believe or understand. But that is what makes this simple adventure stand out on the pages of history as marking the beginning of the end for the great Inca empire. If the Indians had known what was in the minds of the white men, they might have been able to defend themselves and to come to better terms with the invaders. If the Spaniards had been wiser, they could have obtained much of what they desired without so much bloodshed and slaughter. But these were rough times, and conquest was carried out according to a rough and cruel pattern.

PIZARRO MEETS ATAHUALPA

This visit of Candia to the chief of Tumbez is only a single happening. There are other more famous meetings of Spaniards with natives. There is the most famous one of all, when Pizarro finally made his perilous and amazing journey through the mountains and came out at last in that sacred valley. That came several years later. Pizarro had known from Candia's story that he had discovered Peru, but he knew, too, that he could not go on and conquer so rich an empire with the few men of his present company. He went back to Panama and then across the waters to Spain to get backing from the king for his venture.

When he finally returned from that long journey, he had gained little enough in the way of equipment or man power. His next trip south was made with less than two hundred men and twenty-seven horses. But with that small company he made his famous conquest. There was perseverance and hardihood on the Spanish side. The explorer went through incredible hardships as he led his men along impossible trails up, up, up to that lofty valley eleven thousand feet above the sea.

At Cajamarca in the year 1532 the famous meeting took place. Pizarro sent word to the Inca emperor, owner of untold riches and ruler over ten million subjects, whose land he had invaded, to come to meet him; and Atahualpa came. He came in his golden litter, arrayed in his royal robes and with all the rich display to which he was accustomed. He came like a child, showing off his power to these strangers because he was so sure of himself that he thought no harm could come to him. Why should the ruler over a far-reaching empire have any fears of a man with less than two hundred followers, even though that man had also the strange, tall animals on which he rode so proudly?

We all know the sorry outcome of that meeting. Pizarro took Atahualpa captive and demanded for his ransom that his subjects bring at his command gold enough to fill a room. The gold was brought, but it did not free the Indian ruler. He was kept a prisoner by his Spanish conqueror, and met, finally, a cruel death.

That was the famous meeting from which history dates the Spanish conquest. But the fate of the great Inca empire was sealed on that earlier day when a single Spanish knight in armor took his life in his hand and went boldly ashore and saw with his own eyes the rich treasures of gold and silver at Tumbez. There the Old World met the New, and a new order of life began in South America.

IN THE DAYS OF THE INCAS

Children of the Sun

MODERN history in South America begins with the coming to its shores of the Spanish conquistadores and the Portuguese explorers and settlers. We are tempted to think that all South American history began then, and to hurry on from that date to the high point of our story, the freeing of the New World from the Old by the group of famous Liberators. But the Liberators themselves would be the first to tell us that their story had roots that went deep into the past. The causes of their Wars of Independence came from three hundred years of Spanish rule, and their armies were made up of native South Americans, many of them of part-Indian blood whose ancestors had built up proud civilizations before a white man ever set foot on the continent.

A LINE OF KINGS

What figures they would be, these Inca kings, if we could have portraits of them, as we do of the heroes of later days! There would be the legendary Manco, Child of the Sun, sent to earth by his father the Sun, to guide and teach his people. It was he who led the tribe which came to be known by the names of their rulers, the Incas, into the high mountain region of Peru four hundred years before the coming of the Spaniards, and there set up his rule.

He is remembered for giving to his people wise rules for peaceful living and for the training of their youth to defend and enlarge the kingdom. He taught them how to cultivate the soil, and so set them on their way to prosperity. With Manco began the centering of all power in the Inca. He was believed to be of divine ancestry, and the same belief continued for his descendants. From his time on, the position of the ruler was so far above that of his subjects that no man, not even a noble of the highest rank, would venture to enter his presence except in a stooping position, and with a burden on his back to show his submission. In the end, this one-man rule delivered the empire into the hands of the Spaniards, for the common people were so accustomed to obedience that they did not rise up to resist the invaders in time to save themselves or their land. But for the building up of the great Inca empire, the leadership of a line of able kings brought results which could have come in no other way. An Inca could set up and control an orderly society, for he could command the service of every member of his entire kingdom.

Inca Rocca, who was fourth or fifth king after Manco, was remembered for his bridges. He was an energetic ruler who was not content to remain within his own boundaries. But how could he send his warriors northward to conquer neighboring tribes when he and his people were shut into high valleys surrounded by lofty mountain ranges, with deep defiles cutting between the steep slopes and dangerous mountain torrents flowing through them? His answer was to set his people to building the famous swinging bridges with which his name was long associated. They were of osiers or willows, with great strands braided first in threes, then nines, and then twenty-sevens, until there was the floor of a swinging structure over which two or three men could go abreast, with other cables forming the sides and railings. These were fastened from one high spot to another across the ravines and gorges.

In one of the early chronicles there is a mention of the effect of these bridges on tribes who dwelt in the region. Some of these peoples marveled at them and admired them so greatly that they came gladly under Inca Rocca's rule without any fighting, for they felt that a king who could create such a structure was worthy of their submission and service.

Each king did his part in extending the empire, which came by the fourteenth century to stretch fifteen hundred miles north and south, and was about three hundred miles wide at its deepest point and perhaps fifty at its narrowest. This great territory was not won without much fighting, but the marvel was that the people did not give themselves wholly over to war. Under the Incas they carried on a peaceful inner life, even while their warrior members were off fighting. Nor did they practice great cruelty upon those whom they defeated in battle. When

INCA RUINS
No one knows how these huge blocks were set in place
by these early builders.

a tribe was conquered, it was the Inca custom to take a group of their leading men and with them their "gods" or idols, to Cuzco, where the great temple of the Sun God stood. While the men shared freely in the life of the court, the idols were set within the temple. When six months had passed, the men returned to their people, leaving the "gods" behind them. They would have learned how superior the Inca ways and gods were to their own customs, and would go back to convert their own people to the new ways. Such was the Inca way of conquest, and it brought contented peoples within the bounds of the empire.

WAYS OF LIFE

The customs of the Incas are interesting in themselves, but to us they are doubly so because of the help they gave the Spaniards in conquering the country. Pizarro and his men came to a people who were used to authority and accustomed to giving unquestioning obedience. No man worked for himself, but all labor was for the state. All the land belonged to the Inca, and its products were divided into three parts, one third being for the Sun, that is, for the temple worship and the priests, one third for the Inca, which included all the government expenses, and one third for the people. It was a wise and fair division, much better than some of the systems which were being practiced in Europe at that time. Of the people's third, the first portions went to the aged, the sick, and any who were in need. When these persons had been looked after, the men were free to till the lands for their own use and for their families. There were no poor, and no unemployed. The life was that of a moderately contented, hardworking people, but a wholly submissive people, given over to the service of the state.

Remarkable results came out of this fairly peaceful, socialized life. The wiser of the Spaniards declared, within twenty or thirty years of their coming, that they had destroyed a civilization which was, in many ways, far better for the natives than anything which they had brought to them. The common people worked hard, though no harder than the workers on the feudal estates of Europe, but the officials of the empire carried out the system of government with reasonable fairness and justice. Among those of better birth, knowledge flourished. Sons of nobles were trained in the arts and had considerable knowledge of the sciences of mathematics, astronomy, and warfare. Surprisingly, they did not have the art of writing, but used instead an elaborate system of knotted *quipus,* or strings, to carry on their trade and keep all their records. There was a legend that writing had once been discovered but that the priests discouraged its use, telling the ruling Inca that a dreadful pestilence which had visited the region at that time came because the gods were displeased at this new idea. So he followed their advice and forbade its use. At any rate, no written records remain.

But there was tradition, handed down from one generation to the next, and in this keeping of tradition lay one cause of the easy conquest by the Europeans. In the days of Pachacuti the Great, most famous of the Incas, who ruled for more than fifty years at the end of the fourteenth century and into the fifteenth, the word began to be passed along that in the future there would come new Children of the Sun, white people, bearded and very stern, who would rule over the empire. This rumor of change prepared the way for the triumph of the Spaniards.

The Inca life, as they met it, made a great impression on the more thoughtful Spanish leaders in South America. After nearly three centuries, Miranda, the first of our group of heroes of the Wars of Independence, was so impressed by what he had seen and known of this Indian people that he suggested the choice of an Inca emperor as ruler of the vast, independent American empire for which he was working. Even today its glory has not been wholly lost in forgetfulness. The great Indian population of the republics which were once within the Inca empire, Ecuador, Peru, Bolivia, and northern Chile, keep many of the old customs and ideas. They are still the Children of the Sun, as their forefathers were.

THE LAST INCAS

The Indians did not submit to the Spanish conquerors without a struggle. Two more Inca names belong on the roll of honor of South American heroes, for the deeds of these Indian leaders are not forgotten, even though at the time their sacrifice seemed in vain.

At the time of Pizarro's coming, the empire was already weakening. Atahualpa's own claim to the throne was being disputed by one of his brothers, and there had been civil strife between the two rival Incas and their followers. After Atahualpa's death, some members of the royal Inca family were willing to take the offices which the Spaniards gave them and pretend that they were rulers, even though they were only puppets, acting under orders from their conquerors. But there was one young man, a nephew of Atahualpa, who refused. Young Tupac Amaru, who had been born in 1540, eight years after Pizarro's entry into Cuzco, refused to make friends with the Spaniards as his father and brother had done. He went out among the people and made himself their leader, so that they came to see in him the true Inca, Child of the Sun God, who should have been their ruler.

So strong was his following that it finally attracted Spanish notice. The viceroy feared a revolt, and the young man was warned by his friends that he must flee to the mountains for safety. He escaped to the high mountain fastnesses of southern Peru, but hundreds of Indians followed him, prepared to fight under his leadership. The viceroy became deeply disturbed, fearing a general uprising of the Peruvians. Tupac Amaru was driven farther and farther back by the Spanish troops sent to capture him, but still he and a few of his most devoted followers managed again and again to escape into the secret hiding places in the rocks, fighting bravely each time before they retreated. At last a Spanish captain with a few soldiers succeeded in making his way into the Indian camp from the rear. The besieged men were so startled by his sudden appearance in their midst that he was able to take the young Inca captive.

The Spaniards brought Tupac Amaru back to Cuzco, and there had him beheaded in the public square in the presence of a great company of his followers who had braved all dangers to catch a last glimpse of this young man whom they worshiped as their true Inca. Those who looked on said that the wailing of the Indians as the execution took place was a sound never to be forgotten.

Two hundred years passed, and the Spaniards had forgotten the name of this young martyr, when a new Indian leader appeared: another young man of the royal line, fifth in descent from Tupac Amaru. But though they had forgotten, he had not. Trained in the college at Cuzco, this heir of the Incas watched with a sad and bitter heart the sufferings of the Indians who toiled as slaves in the mines and the fields with no hope for the future. He took the name of his ancestor, calling himself Tupac Amaru II, and began to work for his people's betterment. At first, he hoped to gain his ends by peaceful means, petitioning for improvement in the laws regarding the labor of the Indian slaves. But his appeals were unheeded. The poor natives still continued their toil under cruel taskmasters, who flogged and ill-treated them while they forced them to work long hours without respite.

When Tupac Amaru II was twenty years old, he succeeded his father as chief of a province high in the Andes. There he began to plan revolt, and there Indians from all the neighboring provinces flocked to his standard. He did succeed in having one of the local Spanish governors, a brutal tyrant, captured and put to death, and then he moved on towards Cuzco. So strong was his force that the Spanish viceroy became disturbed and sought to negotiate with the Inca leader. Tupac Amaru agreed willingly. This was what he had long desired. Now he could set forth the grievances of his oppressed people with the assurance, as he thought, that they would be considered. But while he was preparing the papers setting forth these complaints, the viceroy was gathering a Spanish army. The whole Indian population of Peru was joining the revolt, and the Spanish officials were genuinely alarmed.

In February, 1781, the army marched against the Inca leader, sending in advance the message that all negotiations were refused. "If you will surrender now, your torture will be less," the letter said in conclusion. But the Indians were in no mood to surrender. Thousands of them had assembled by this time. Some historians estimate the forces of Tupac Amaru II as two hundred thousand men. The fighting that followed was fearful. No struggle in South American history was more bloody or barbarous. But the Indians had no chance, in spite of their numbers, against the well-armed, well-trained Spanish soldiers. Thousands of the aborigines were killed, and Tupac Amaru and his family were taken captive.

On May 18, 1781, all members of the family and then the Inca himself were executed in the most cruel manner as an example to the Indians of the impossibility of revolt against the governing powers. But the wiser Spaniards who saw this horrible death of the young leader were filled with forebodings. The ways of the Spanish Inquisition which had spread terror in Europe were being copied on the American continent, and there were those who knew that there could be but one end to such a struggle. A native people could not be oppressed forever, and there were the grievances of the white men and those of mixed blood in the colonies, as well as of these humbler workers and servants of Indian descent. The Inca rebellion was one sign of the future move towards independence.

THE YEARS BETWEEN

IT would be unfair to let a single story of a native revolt remain as our only impression of colonial days in the Spanish-American empire. Spain ruled her great American possessions for three hundred years before their people sought complete independence from the mother country. Her viceroys and captains general and other officials did much good service to the people, and gradually opened up to trade and contact with the outer world the remote inland sections as well as the coastal areas. The Jesuits established their missions among the Indians and carried on schools and churches. One could tell many pleasant tales of their service to the simple aboriginals, as well as of the work of the wiser and more efficient viceroys who carried on the government and built up the cities. But that part of the story of the continent does not belong in our tale, for none of these men are South America's own heroes. In spite of their years of service and residence on the American continent, they remained Spanish, returning gladly to the homeland when their terms of office were over. The colonies were the property of the king, and he sent out his own men to rule them. The Spanish-Americans who were born on this side of the water instead of in Europe had little or no chance for advancement.

That is why we find few native leaders during this long period of colonial rule.

Out of this treatment of the creole class, which was made up of families of as pure Spanish descent as many of the officials sent out from Spain, came the discontent which led to the movement of the colonies for independence. The young men of the early nineteenth century were impatient of such treatment and eager for revolution and national independence. We shall see this in the lives of our "liberators." Spain allowed these families which settled in the colonies to acquire and hold great areas of land, thus giving them power. But she denied to their sons either social equality or government positions. She bled the colonies, too, for money, and restrained their trade by aggravating rules. They could not trade back and forth with one another, but only with the mother country. Indeed, creoles, that is, colonials of native birth, could not even move freely from one part of the continent to another without going to the trouble of getting royal permission, which was often refused. Nor was the trade with Spain open trade in which all could join. All commerce was managed by a few companies which were under control of the Spanish government and handled both buying and selling at an enormous profit. In both Spanish and Portuguese colonies there were tax and trade restrictions far in excess of those which stirred our North American colonies to revolt from English rule.

The revolutionary ideas which were inspired by our

own American Revolution and the French Revolution found a ready response in South America in the years which followed those great national movements. With the Wars of Independence of the early nineteenth century the heroic age of South America begins. The men who led the fight for freedom were American-born and American-bred, for all their Spanish training and background. In them we see the first truly American leaders of the southern continent. They were not only liberators of their countries but also builders of the New World, founders of the republics of today.

MIRANDA, FORERUNNER OF INDEPENDENCE

SOLDIER OF FORTUNE AND PATRIOT

"That man has a sacred fire in his soul."—Napoleon

IN the national pantheon of Venezuela there stands, next to the statue of Bolívar, a memorial to Miranda bearing this inscription: "He took part in three political movements of his age: the struggle for independence of the United States of North America; the French Revolution; and the emancipation of South America."

No other man in history has such a record. Bolívar,

South America's greatest Liberator, was not born till 1783, the year of the close of the American Revolution. But Francisco de Miranda was already twenty-seven years old at that time, and had spent two years in service to our cause as a Spanish army officer, when Spain, as an ally of France, was drawn into our conflict on the American side.

So in his own picturesque person Miranda bridges the gap between our American Revolution and the South American Wars of Independence, and helps to make us see them as parts of one great fifty-year struggle of the Americas to free themselves from Old World domination. In 1924 there was a celebration in the city of Washington of the hundredth anniversary of the final battle of the South American Wars, the Battle of Ayacucho, and a South American statesman, giving the address, reminded his hearers that the fight for American independence began with the Battle of Lexington on April 19, 1775, and did not end till this Battle of Ayacucho was fought, high among the mountains of Peru, on December 9, 1824. That is the way this South American statesman saw his All-America history, and that is the way Miranda would have seen it. There were more than twenty years between the end of the one struggle and the beginning of the other, but Miranda bridged those years by his own devoted work. During that entire time he was laboring in Europe for the cause of South American independence and so earning the title by which he has since become known, the title of "Forerunner of South American Independence."

YOUTH AS A SOLDIER

The boyhood of Francisco de Miranda followed a pattern that was quite usual for a young Venezuelan. Born in Caracas on June 9, 1756, he was educated in the schools of that city and then went overseas to Spain when he was sixteen years old. His ancestry reached back to Spain in a long line of men of noble birth who had often held official positions under the kings. His father, Sebastian de Miranda, had emigrated to South America in the middle of the eighteenth century, become a merchant in Caracas, married Francisca de Espinosa in 1751, and served under the Spanish Captain General of Venezuela as head of a volunteer militia company.

Young Francisco chose to be a soldier, and his father seconded his desire by buying for him, for the sum of eight thousand pesos, a captaincy in a Spanish regiment. In this service the boy learned the military arts which were to make him, for the rest of his life, a welcome volunteer in any war, whether in the Old World or the New. Even in his youth, however, his soldierly career was neither smooth nor serene. He was a handsome, high-spirited lad with a brilliant mind, who attracted notice wherever he went and was often in trouble with his superiors. This was partly due to his own temperament, but partly, too, to the position in which he found himself as a young colonial from South America. There was a sharp line drawn between those members of old Spanish families who were born and brought up in Spain, and those who came from homes set up for one generation or longer in the New World. No proud youth from the colonies who had the best Spanish blood in his veins could fail to resent being treated as a social inferior by the haughty young Spanish-born aristocrats with whom he lived and studied.

Nowhere are Spain's blunders in dealing with her colonial possessions more evident than in her treatment of the young men who came to the "homeland" to be educated. She sowed the seeds of discontent even while she was teaching them the military skill which they were so soon to use against her. During long, dull periods of life in Spanish garrisons, young Miranda was more than ready to read every book setting forth the new and revolutionary doctrines of the "Rights of Man" and "Liberty and Equality" which were current at that time.

The boy saw active service soon after his enlistment, being sent to Africa with his regiment to fight the Moors. One of the routine official reports of that period speaks of Captain Miranda as "possessing valor, great application, and undoubted capacity," but states that he "ought to display more prudence." That was what he seems never to have succeeded in doing. So he was frequently under discipline, which was more or less severe according to the disposition of the men in authority over him. There are tales of his being confined in a military fortress for a time —and of his reading meanwhile all the books, military, literary, and of every sort, on which he could lay hands.

It was in 1780 that Captain Miranda was first sent across the seas to American waters. France and Spain were beginning to give active help to the American cause, and Miranda came with his regiment to Cuba. There he did good service as our allies harassed the English in the Caribbean waters and in Cuba, Florida, and Georgia. He was even entrusted with important secret missions, and won his rank as colonel following the successful entry of the Spanish forces into Pensacola.

Cuba was at that time a hotbed of Spanish political intrigue. There were suspicions and accusations of illegal smuggling, of trade plots for money, with bribes to officers in the army, and of disloyalty to one faction or another. The high official whose aide-de-camp Miranda had been fell into disfavor with government officials higher up, and Miranda was involved. His friends advised that he get out of the country at once, to avoid threatened discipline and imprisonment, and to give them time during his absence to present his case at court in Spain. Under an assumed name he slipped away secretly on a boat which landed him in Newbern, North Carolina, in June, 1783.

TRAVELS IN THE UNITED STATES
1783-1784

Miranda seems always to belong to us of the United States more than does any other hero of the South American Wars, because of his service on our side during these last years of the Revolution, and because of the year and a half which he spent at this time in the newly established United States. We have many accounts, in letters and diaries written by Englishmen and Frenchmen, of life here as it was lived immediately following the Revolution, but there is something different in the viewpoint of this South American. He traveled from city to city, observing our ways closely and being entertained by many of our most distinguished men, and all the while he kept a faithful diary, according to the custom of those days.

A portrait done shortly after this sojourn shows Miranda as a typical Spanish-American gentleman of the period. He was of medium height, with piercing eyes, prominent nose, high forehead, and dark hair which was powdered and worn long with the ends fastened in a pigtail which was tucked in underneath. In the portrait he is shown handsomely and fashionably dressed in a frilled shirt, white waistcoat, and dark cloth coat. During his many visits in the capitals of Europe, as well as during this American tour, the colonel was very much the society man, devoted to the ladies and acceptable as a guest in the homes where he was entertained. He sought out people, partly from a natural liking for them, and partly for the sake of his beloved cause—the freeing of the South American colonies from Spanish rule. Dr. Priestley, the famous scientist, who met him at this time, tells that Miranda remarked to him that his aim was "rather to converse with Men than to see Countries."

One of the early entries in the diary records a dinner with General Washington in Philadelphia when the General was on his way to resign his commission as commander-in-chief of the American army. He found Washington's manner "circumspect, taciturn, and inexpressive."

FRANCISCO DE MIRANDA
1756–1816
Plaza del Panteón, Caracas.

The calm of our stately leader was not likely to appeal to the demonstrative and emotional young Venezuelan.

Miranda himself was all afire, as all these South American patriots were, with their cause. "He loves liberty," commented one of his hosts, "with an ardor that would do honor to the freest State in the world." A young boy in whose home he visited remembered twenty years later that Miranda appeared to him "the most extraordinary and wonderfully energetic man" whom he had ever seen. "His darling theme," he said, "was the prospect of revolutionizing the Spanish province of South America. . . . While commenting on these subjects with great vehemence of enthusiasm . . . and in a rapid, impassioned and commanding eloquence," he paced the room with "giant strides, with his whole frame in motion." Thomas Paine, author of the pamphlet *Common Sense* which had done much to arouse American sentiment in 1776, described him as a "man of talents and enterprise, and the whole of his life . . . a life of adventure."

It is interesting that Miranda was somewhat disturbed by what he considered an excess of democracy in the newly formed nation. "The spirit of republicanism was so strong," he wrote in his diary, "that the coachman who drove the stage, and all the other guests sat together at the same table . . ." He found no small difficulty, he remarked, in arranging to have his own servant eat by himself.

The Venezuelan talked South American independence in season and out with all the leaders of American opinion whom he could meet. He even went so far as to work out with General Henry Knox, whose military skill in the American Revolution he had greatly admired, a somewhat startling plan for raising a paid army of five thousand soldiers in New England, enlisting them for a five-year term in a campaign to "revolutionize the Spanish Indies." A similar plan was discussed with Alexander Hamilton, and the list of probable officers was made up and put on paper.

Reading of these arrangements, we feel as if something was due to happen almost at once, and the freedom from Spain to be won by force shortly. But Colonel Miranda had no such expectation of an immediate revolt. He was convinced that the break-up of the Spanish empire must come through aid to the oppressed colonials by some foreign power. They could not gain their freedom by their own military or political efforts on their own shores. He had hopes of such foreign aid because of the unsettled state of Europe at this time. England had lost her North American colonies, and the nations were looking with envy at the rich colonies to the south which kept the coffers of the Spanish king filled with gold.

We have a letter written to Miranda as far back as 1781 or 1782, when he was still in the Spanish army in Cuba, which shows how the young revolutionists in Venezuela shared Miranda's conviction of the need of foreign support and counted on him to get it for them. Its final sentences are worth quoting because they show, too, the attitude of these would-be rebels to Miranda.

You are the eldest son from whom the Motherland expects this important service:—we are the younger brothers who on bended knees and with arms outstretched beseech this of you for the love of God! At the first signal we are ready to follow you as our leader to the end and to shed the last drop of our blood in great and honorable enterprises! . . . We shall not take a single step except by your advice; for in your prudence we have placed all our hopes.

They did not know, nor did Miranda, that more than twenty years were to pass before he returned to his country and led such a revolt on his native soil.

After a year and a half in the United States, Miranda sailed for Europe. He was going, by his own word, to complete his "defective education" in military and other matters by an extensive tour of Europe. During his journeyings he intended to enlist all the help he could for the revolution which he hoped to bring about—and then to lead!

HIS WORK ABROAD
1784-1805

Looking back, we can see that Miranda's greatest work for freedom was done in the years when he must have seemed to himself to have been accomplishing least, years when he met with one disappointment and failure after another. "That man has a sacred fire in his soul," Napoleon Bonaparte remarked after an evening spent as one of a group of guests in the Venezuelan's apartment in Paris. That fire was what kept the flame of interest in the cause of South American independence alive in the capitals of Europe and in England during long, weary, disappointing years. Time and again his work must have seemed to him utterly fruitless, as one hopeful project after another failed. Yet, when we read the lives of the younger patriot leaders, of Bolívar, of San Martín, of O'Higgins, and others, we find that their enthusiasm was kindled and rekindled, not in South America, but at Miranda's fireside in London or at meetings of one of his chain of secret societies in Europe.

The tale of the man's travels is astonishing. Soon after his arrival in Europe from the United States he went as far as Russia and there became a personal favorite of the reigning Czarina, Catherine II, who was given to having handsome young courtiers as her favorites. During all his journeyings he was closely watched by the Spanish government, and well he might be! However gay his life might appear to be, or however deeply he was involved in other political concerns, he never for a single moment forgot his cause. If any government anywhere was at odds with Spain, there Miranda was at its headquarters, presenting his plea for help for his fellow-countrymen and suggesting how simple it would be to deprive Spain of its rich colonies by giving support to the would-be revolutionists.

The French Revolution came in those years, and Miranda was placed in command of a division of the French army under General Dumouriez. Rising to the rank of

General, he won distinction by capturing the city of Antwerp. But Dumouriez was proved a traitor, and Miranda was recalled to Paris to stand trial on the charge of being party to the Frenchman's treasonable plans. At first acquitted and then suspected again, he spent a year and a half in prison. But he weathered these political storms and lived near Paris from the date of his release from prison in 1795 until 1798, when he went to England. There he presented one plan and another to Sir William Pitt and others high in the government counsels who were quite ready to consider schemes directed against Spanish control of American territory. Money allowances were granted to him by the British from time to time, and he seems to have gone from poverty to a life of ease and back again as fortune favored or deserted him at the moment.

One of his plans is interesting because it reminds us how all America was still in the making in those days. Miranda outlined for Pitt's consideration, a scheme for a huge new state which was to be bounded on the north by part of the Mississippi river, and was to include all of Mexico and of Central and South America (except for Portuguese-owned Brazil and the British, French and Dutch Guianas) from the Isthmus to Cape Horn. This great state, of which he dreamed, was to have at its head an Inca emperor, descendant of the Incas of old. Miranda reported that the Indian population in this Spanish-claimed region numbered about six million, while there were probably about five million persons of Spanish blood, mixed birth, and negroes.

Self-interest was the argument which he always used with the Englishmen. According to this plan the territory which he was including in his new American empire was producing annually gold, silver, tobacco, sugar, cacao, and other goods to the amount of fifty-five million pesos. He was enough of a business man and diplomat to talk of this South American treasure, but his own interest was always in the cause of liberty.

Napoleon's movements defeated one of the most likely projects for English help to the South American revolutionists. The British statesmen seem to have been almost on the point of lending some aid to Miranda and his friends, when Napoleon marched his armies over into Spain. That changed the look of things entirely. England must stand, outwardly at least, with the loyalist government in Spain, lest the dictator gain so much power on the Continent that he dare to attempt to cross the English Channel and attack the British Isles. The English might have no special love for Spain, but they did not have any desire to have the rich Spanish Indies fall into French hands. The British cabinet member to whom it fell to tell Miranda of the change of plan was so disturbed over disappointing the Venezuelan, after his hopes had been raised so high, that he decided to do it outdoors instead of at his house, and the two walked for hours while Miranda poured forth his bitterness.

The outcome for Miranda was an immediate return to

the United States. The disturbed conditions in Europe were having a profound effect on this side of the water. The Spanish government had been at odds with our own, with some threat of war. There might be the long-desired support for his plan in Washington, where the huge territory included in the Louisiana Purchase had been recently acquired from France, and there was watchful concern over the fate of the colonies to the south. So after an absence of eighteen years Miranda returned to this country and picked up the talk of plans almost as if he had never been away.

BACK TO VENEZUELA

A new nation is brought into existence

FROM the moment of his return to the United States Miranda began to work definitely for revolution in Venezuela. It was obvious to others than himself that some change was due to come soon in South America. The days of Spanish rule were numbered.

As nearly as we can gather from the cautious records which remain concerning the Venezuelan's reception here, our government did not intend either to hinder, or too openly to help, any revolutionary movement. President Jefferson, before whom Miranda laid his plans (as he did also before his old friend Henry Knox and James Madison, at this time Secretary of State), spoke freely of his own desire to see the whole New World "advance to complete independence," but feared that he had been born too soon to live to see that happen.

THE LEANDER EXPEDITION FROM NEW YORK
1806

Miranda's brief stay in the United States led to an expedition, a strange and tragic misadventure, which makes one link between North Americans and the cause of South American independence.

With money obtained partly from New Yorkers and partly through English sources, General Miranda bought, early in the year 1806, a vessel of one hundred and eighty-seven tons, the *Leander,* and had it provisioned and armed. The way recruits were obtained for this expedition gives a curious picture of the unsettled condition of the times. Wars were going on in Europe and spreading their influence to American waters. Smuggling and filibustering parties were at work along the Atlantic seacoast and in the West Indies. Miranda's agents were able to enlist two hundred young men, most of them American citizens, who went aboard with the vaguest possible information as to the purpose of the voyage, thinking that it was some sort of secret mission, approved by the government, with a prospect of some fighting, and the hope of seizure of treasure or perhaps of military glory.

Few of the recruits saw their leader until they were several days out at sea. Then the General appeared on deck, a courtly soldier, though strangely dressed in a red lounging robe and slippers. One of the party described him thus:

> He is about five feet ten inches high. His limbs are well proportioned; his whole frame is stout and active. His complexion is dark, florid and healthy. His eyes are hazel-colored, but not of the darkest hue. They are piercing, quick and intelligent, expressing more of the severe than the mild feelings. He has good teeth, which he takes much care to keep clean. His nose is large and handsome, rather of the English than the Roman cast. His chest is square and prominent. His hair is gray and he wears it

tied long behind with powder. He has strong gray whiskers growing on the outer edges of his ears, as large as most Spaniards have on their cheeks. . . . When sitting he is never perfectly still; his foot or hand must be kept moving to keep time with his mind which is always in exercise. . . . He is an eminent example of temperance. A scanty or bad meal is never regarded by him as a subject of complaint.

He is a courtier and gentleman in his manners. Dignity and grace preside in his movements. . . . In discourse he is logical in the management of his thoughts. He appears conversant on all subjects.

During the days at sea the General proceeded to captivate the young men by tales of his adventures in Europe and by his picturing of the great enterprise ahead. Before the vessel touched at its first port, most of the boys—and they were hardly more than boys—were ready to enlist as volunteers in a revolutionary army to fight for South American freedom.

Then followed confusion and tragedy. The *Leander* and its two smaller companion boats were delayed a month in Santo Domingo. By the time they reached Puerto Cabello, Venezuela, the Spanish authorities were warned of their coming and on the watch. The transports, with sixty of the Americans, were promptly captured by Spanish warships, but the *Leander,* with Miranda aboard, succeeded in getting away. The captives were taken ashore and thrown into Spanish fortresses. Ten were hanged at once; the others were kept in prison until most of them met a slow death. A monument erected by Venezuelans a few years ago shows that the sacrifice of these young North Americans has not been forgotten. Those who suffered death on that first horrible day were reported to have met their fate with the "most undaunted resolution."

Miranda prolonged the expedition a few months, coming back and taking the town of Coro on the coast in western Venezuela. But he was bitterly disappointed by his reception there. He had expected that the moment he landed there would be an uprising of native-born South American patriots, rallying around his standard. He had counted, too, on assistance from the English vessels which were in near-by waters. But there was no such response. It has been suggested that perhaps it was his talk of expected British backing which made the natives hesitate. They desired, above all else, to be freed from certain Spanish injustices which they deeply resented, but they did not wish to come under another foreign government. Miranda was forced to withdraw.

THE CALL HOME

Miranda returned to London in 1807 a bitterly disappointed man. He had dreamed for years of the hour when he should set foot on his native soil and lead his fellow-countrymen to independence. But he had crossed the seas and made such a landing with no response from them. Now he settled down again in his lodgings in Grafton Street, off Tottenham Court Road, and the group of disgruntled Spanish-Americans began once more to gather and plot and talk.

Success was nearer than they dreamed—and from the hands of the last man in the world who would have been expected to open the door of opportunity for a free America. Napoleon set out at this time to conquer Spain, and in 1808 he forced the weak, elderly king, Charles IV, to abdicate, placing his own brother, Joseph Bonaparte, on the throne, to rule Spain and her colonies. But the Spanish people rose up in protest. All over the peninsula, at that time, there were organized patriotic local councils, called *juntas*. These declared their loyalty to Ferdinand VII, the imprisoned son of Charles IV, and to the Regency which the royalist Spaniards established to carry on the government on his behalf and express their defiance of the Bonapartes.

The events in Venezuela were dramatic. A French brig was sent across the seas to carry to the colonies the news that Joseph Bonaparte was on the throne of Spain. While Juan de Casas, captain general at Caracas, was receiving the two uniformed French officials, who had gone to his palace from their boat to carry the message, the news of their coming spread in the town. An excited mob, of whom young Simón Bolívar, lately returned from Europe, was one, gathered in the streets.

A French king to rule over them, they were saying indignantly—had they come to that pass? Spain might be accepting a Bonaparte as king, but not Caracas. When the Spanish captain-general returned from escorting his guests to their lodging, he found the audience room of his palace invaded by this company from the streets, who were shouting: "Long live King Ferdinand! Down with the French Usurper!"

It is a strange picture. Miranda might well marvel when the news of this scene came to him. Here were young Venezuelan patriots, like Simón Bolívar and his brother, who had been holding secret meetings outside Caracas to further the cause of independence from Spain. Yet they were joining with the mob in their demand for loyalty to King Ferdinand. They welcomed the break in Spain's power, but chose to move cautiously as if in complete agreement with the opposition to the French ruler. It would be time enough later to move the one step further and put forth the cry, "The old king or none!" Then the next step would be independence.

The Caracas mob proceeded next to the lodging of the French envoys, who did not at all enjoy the situation in which they found themselves. Hastily, under escort of a few of De Casas' soldiers, they departed to the boat on which they had just arrived. That was the end of Napoleon's announcement to the colonies. The frightened French messengers little knew, as they sailed back home, that they had given the signal which was to start the movement for home rule in the overseas colonies.

But Miranda knew. When the news of this happening came to him, he sat down in his London lodgings and wrote a letter to the patriot group in Caracas, a letter which was read at one of its secret meetings at the San Mateo home of Simón Bolívar.

"Spain," he wrote, "has no longer a king. She is split

in two. . . . A civil war is raging. The colonies are ripe for self-government! Send your agents to me, and together we will work out the future of the new continent."

Within a few months young Simón Bolívar with two companions was on his way to England as the delegate of the Caracas *junta* to try to get British help against the French Bonaparte. In London, Lord Wellesley, British Secretary for Foreign Affairs, received the young officers cordially and listened to their story. His answer was what might have been expected. The message which they had brought from the *junta* had said nothing of independence from Spain, but had professed loyalty to Ferdinand. The young men had spoken as if their Caracas *junta* wished recognition as an independent government ruling Venezuela, but there was no such word in the written message. Britain's answer was that if the colonists were attacked from France, her troops would come to their aid. The young delegates could expect no more, but this was not enough to satisfy them.

Bolívar went out from that interview to another which he had been anticipating for a long time. He had been warned not to go to General Miranda, for the old army officer was not popular in Venezuela since the *Leander* expedition two years earlier. Nor would it help the struggling young government to seem to be having dealings with a man who had spent a generation working against Spanish rule. But Bolívar did not heed these cautions. He and his friend López Méndez, a fellow delegate, went to see Miranda, and Bolívar told him that the time for action had come.

Doubtless Bolívar in his enthusiasm and impatience of delay made the old warrior think that the patriot cause was stronger than it was. General Miranda accused him later of such misrepresentation. But the three young men were persuasive and the older man was eager to make the move for which he had been working so long.

In the fall of 1810 Miranda and Bolívar left England. Bolívar, being an official delegate from the Caracas *junta,* returned on the British warship *Sapphire.* The two other delegates, Méndez and Bello, remained in London, taking up their residence in Miranda's quarters. There they were to remain for some years, representing the South American cause with the British people and raising money and enlisting men. Miranda came with some of his followers on the British ship *Avon,* landing in La Guaira, the seaport of Caracas, nine days after Bolívar's arrival.

STARTING THE REPUBLIC

There are stirring scenes now all along Miranda's path.

The first is in the harbor of La Guaira, off Caracas, on the morning of December 14, 1810. General Miranda stands on the deck of the *Avon,* a striking figure in his old French uniform, the sky-blue coat, white trousers, and tricolor sash of the Republic. He is returning to his native land after thirty-seven years of life abroad, save for the few weeks of the ill-fated *Leander* expedition. He is only fifty-four years old, but illness and hardship have so aged him that he appears to be at least sixty, with his gray hair and gray side whiskers.

In the city there has been the news of his coming, and the *junta* of Caracas, now its governing body, has desired to give him a suitable welcome. But its members are not entirely happy in so doing. They are still trying to steer a safe middle course between Spanish loyalty and local independence. They know full well that it will not help them in this attempt to be entertaining a man who has spent much of his life working against Spain in the capitals of Europe. Yet Bolívar and his friends have persuaded them that the General's help is needed in their future struggle for complete independence.

The *junta* has done its part well. A messenger goes out from the shore to hand to the returning hero a proclamation of welcome. In it there is no suggestion of disloyalty to Spain, but a statement that the "ancient tyranny" of the former government has now been succeeded by a Spanish rule which has for its sole aim the happiness and well being of the people of Venezuela. (As a matter of fact, the Regency had recognized the existing dissatisfaction and had made conditions much better for the colonists.)

Miranda receives this paper, reads it, and then steps into the boat which is to take him ashore. Cheers rise from the waiting crowd on the beach and wharves as he stands, arms folded on his chest, at the bow of the small rowboat.

A MOUNTAIN TRAIL

Today, as in the days of the Liberators, supplies must be
carried across the mountain ranges on pack animals.

The committee is waiting at the pier and gives him an effusive welcome as he lands.

Bolívar, who had left London at about the same time but arrived a few days earlier, is there with the other patriots. The others fall back as these two mount horses and start together along the steep trail which winds up the mountain and then down on the other side to the city of Caracas, twenty miles away. The scenery is beautiful, but the General may well be wondering how he is to transport armies and their supplies on these narrow mountain paths where no wheeled vehicle has ever been used.

They ride together, with the welcoming escort before and behind, and at the journey's end Miranda enters the city on his beautiful white horse to the shouts of an immense crowd of enthusiastic citizens. That night he goes to the house of Bolívar as his guest.

The next weeks and months are hard ones for the General. If we could follow him about, we should see him finding it difficult to fit into this homeland from which he has been so long away. He who has served in the superbly trained armies of Europe looks at the small companies of militia and the ill-disciplined groups of soldiers and is appalled. "Where," he asks Bolívar bitterly, "are the armies which are worthy of a general of my dignity and reputation?" It is more than a pettish complaint. He knows enough to fear for the results of a campaign with only this army. Yet the brusque criticisms which he is at little pains to hide are irritating to the eager, proud young men. He seems like a foreigner to them, and he takes no care to hide his distaste for native foods and customs. Whenever he can, he spends his time with the French officers stationed in the city, feeling more at home with them than with the native Venezuelans.

Yet when he exerts himself, he can be his courteous, energetic, eloquent self, preaching of the free nation which will shortly be established. He succeeds in getting himself elected as a delegate to the new Venezuelan Congress, and we see him seated at the opening meeting on March second, 1811, while the oath is taken by all its members to defend the rights of Ferdinand VII (still in prison) and oppose any other ruler who might aim to exercise authority in the Venezuelan provinces. But from that Congress the heralds go out on that first day to announce in the streets that "a new nation has been brought into existence." By July the discussion becomes open as to the wisdom of a declaration of complete independence from war-ridden Spain.

The Congress is, in those days, a distressingly timid body, and Miranda's satisfaction comes in the evening meetings of the active Patriotic Society which is working towards revolution and complete independence of Spain. Here he is thoroughly at home; here he is an honored leader.

On July fourth, 1811, Miranda is in the chair presiding over its meeting, when young Bolívar makes his maiden speech. There are those, he says, who have counseled waiting on the policy of Spain. But what does it matter how Spain is carrying on dealings with Napoleon if the colony is resolved to be free? He finishes a fiery talk with a motion that a committee from the Patriotic Society present to the Congress its urgent desire for immediate action. Miranda puts the motion, and it is carried with enthusiasm on this Fourth of July, the thirty-fifth anniversary of the Declaration of Independence of the North American colonies.

When the matter is debated the next day in the National Congress, Miranda rises to speak on its behalf. His words are always heeded, for he speaks with eloquence and with the authority given him by his long experience. Other delegates argue that such a step is inconsistent with the oath they have taken to support Ferdinand VII. The reply is promptly made that the ruling family in Spain has practically sold all of Spanish America to Napoleon. How then can such an oath be binding? Another delegate expresses the fear that Venezuela with only a million inhabitants is not strong enough to take such a step. Miranda leaps to his feet. He can use the knowledge gained during his extensive foreign travels to answer that objection. The United States, he reminds them, did not have three million white inhabitants when she "perfected her immortal enterprise." The Swiss Republic had only two million when it declared for independence, and it and other countries even smaller have been able to maintain their liberty successfully. Moreover, Venezuela is not wholly alone. She has neighbor states which might take the same position.

Soon after this speech the vote is taken, and it is almost unanimous in favor of declaring the colony free. The word spreads from the audience chamber to the street, and the city goes wild with delight. Venezuela is to be an independent nation. Jubilant young men dash through the streets tearing down the portraits of Ferdinand VII and trampling them underfoot. Miranda has lived to see the beginnings of a republican government in his native land.

These are the great moments in Miranda's life, moments when his presence serves his birthplace well by giving courage and confidence to the younger leaders. The flag of Spain is lowered from the public buildings, and the patriots choose for the new nation the flag which Miranda had flown in 1806 from the masthead of the *Leander*. It is a tricolor of red, blue, and yellow, the colors which are used still as the national colors of Venezuela, Colombia, and Ecuador. The yellow, Miranda says, stands for the golden sands of South America, the blue for the high longings of the patriots, and the red for the blood shed to win independence. The shedding of that blood is— alas!—to begin almost at once.

FROM VICTORY TO DEFEAT

"The Judgment of God has come upon you!"

MIRANDA was given command of the army of the new republic, and had to act almost at once to quell the royalist uprisings, both in Caracas and the city of Valencia. He did not take the least pains to conceal his disappointment in the hastily assembled army. They were ill-trained and undisciplined—a painful contrast to the fine soldiery whom he had led in Europe. He had spoken sharply to young Bolívar about them during his first months in South America, sneering at the young man's defense of them as fearless fighters, who would be ready and eager to obey to the death when they were properly trained. Now, finding Bolívar at the head of the troop of Aragua militia, Miranda declared that he would not serve if the young upstart of a colonel had a post.

There was bound to be a break between the old warrior and the young Venezuelan, who was becoming more and more a leader among the patriots. On this occasion Bolívar tore off the insignia of his rank and declared that he would go as a common soldier, and Miranda allowed him to do so. But in the battle of Valencia which followed shortly, Bolívar fought with such bravery and led the men who rallied around him with such success that when the victory was won, Miranda was forced to restore him to his former position as colonel of the militia. The favorable citation to "Colonel Simón Bolívar" was, however, almost the last good word that the General ever had for him. Soon he was describing his former aide as a "dangerous youth."

How Miranda would have succeeded with the rebellion if he had had only the Spanish forces to reckon with is something no man can say. A more sinister element, a terrible earthquake, came into the tense situation.

THE EARTHQUAKE OF 1812

On Holy Thursday, March 26, 1812, when the people were attending the churches in preparation for Good Friday, there began to be alarming rumblings up in the mountains. The strange, awful sound grew, and the earth began to shake. Worshipers in the churches rushed for the doors, but before they could reach them the heavy rafters were crashing down and the outer walls were falling in upon them. Along the streets houses were falling, crushing those within, while those who could escape were rushing to the open squares there to kneel and pray for deliverance.

The disaster had come on the church anniversary of the day when the Spanish captain general had been deposed in Caracas. The priests, who were royalists opposed to the people's movement for liberty, went about among the frightened people holding their crosses aloft and commanding them to pray for forgiveness and mercy.

"This is the Judgment of God," they shouted. "Two years ago Caracas drove away the representatives of His Holy Majesty, the King of Spain! Now behold the Judgment of God that has come upon you."

From the mourning people rose in terrified response the cry, "Down with the Republic! Let us acknowledge the King! This is the Judgment of God!"

By a strange turn of fate Nature did seem to have turned against the patriots. The regions where they were in power suffered most in the earthquake, while the royalist centers on the coast and farther inland were scarcely harmed. Six hundred soldiers of the Republic were killed in the collapse of the Caracas barracks; another six hundred were lost on the road along which they were marching, as it caved in and the ground swallowed them up. Twelve thousand people lost their lives.

The loss of men was serious, but it was as nothing to the effect on the morale of the people. In a letter dated four days after the tragedy, an English captain, stationed on a ship in the harbor, wrote home that this would be a death blow to General Miranda and his followers if the supporters of the Spanish king were wise enough to follow up their advantage at once. This the Spanish did. A former officer in their navy, Domingo Monteverde, had arrived at Coro, a royalist seacoast fort which had been out of the path of the disaster, and offered his services to the Spanish leaders there. They welcomed him gladly and put him at the head of an army which marched against the forces of the patriots.

A LONG YEAR

There followed a series of engagements and counter-engagements in which Miranda, to whom the Congress had granted extraordinary powers, acted chiefly on the defensive, with Monteverde pushing his men back and taking one town and another. It is difficult to get a clear picture of what was in Miranda's mind in these days. He had tried for more than a year to build up an army, but apparently he felt that the infant Republic could not survive against Spanish attack without some help from an outside nation. He believed that Venezuela's best help was likely to come from France, and he is said to have opened negotiations for such aid. At any rate, he was surrounded by French officers whose presence the Venezuelan army officers bitterly resented. There were money troubles which the official in charge of money affairs tried to solve by issues of paper money. Miranda issued a proclamation freeing all slaves for conscription in the republican army, and brought down thereby a flood of complaints upon his head. The owners were to be repaid in paper money "as soon as possible," and they considered the paper money of little or no value. The rains came early that June of 1812, and the soldiers' camps were soon afloat, while their marches were carried on through rivers of red mud. The truth of the matter seems to be that Miranda was trying to perform a task for which he was at this time ill-suited, even if he could have carried it through when he was a younger man. He had never had to gather raw recruits and drill them, nor did he know how to inspire his men and lead them. He dared not send out an ill-trained army against the enemy, little realizing that those men, however lacking in the military arts, would have fought their way through in this rough country with which they were so familiar.

Towards the end of June there was a victory for the patriots. Monteverde made two attacks on the fortified town of La Victoria, the patriot army headquarters, and was defeated with heavy loss of life among his men. This was the time, if there was to be one, for the republican army to sally forth and take the offensive. But General Miranda delayed in spite of the impatience of the officers of the army. He was still sending representatives to foreign powers, with letters seeking assistance for the republic. Meanwhile, it was his apparent intention to hold his gains and play a waiting game.

The Fifth of July came, and he gave a simple dinner to one hundred of his officers in honor of the first anniversary of the Declaration of Independence of Venezuela. The story of that dinner was told many years later by a distinguished Venezuelan, who was at that time about to leave on a mission from Miranda to the United States, seeking aid. When the meal was over, the General drew him apart and began to talk to him about his trip to the United States, telling of Jefferson and Adams, and other prominent Americans, and of the weakness and strength of each one. He was to give him letters of introduction to all these men, whom he knew so well. They were drinking their coffee together when a colonel in the army appeared at the door of the room and announced the arrival of dispatches. General Miranda withdrew, saying that he would be back shortly, and when the delay became long, this gentleman followed to his secretary's office.

There he found the General pacing back and forth from one end of the room to the other. Three other men were with him, but no one was speaking. One of the three was pounding the palm of one hand on the other; another was sitting crestfallen, sunk in thought; the third was standing like a statue beside the desk. With a fear of what he would hear, the gentleman turned to the General and asked what had happened. There was no reply. He asked again, and then a third time. After a considerable time the General took a paper out of his waistcoat pocket saying (in French), "Venezuela is wounded to the heart." "Never," reported the gentleman later, "shall I forget the picture which these venerable patriots of American emancipation presented in that critical moment, struck down by the intensity of the present blow, and the foreboding of the calamities which were likely to follow to afflict unhappy Venezuela."

The paper was a brief note from Simón Bolívar, who had been sent away from the scene of the main fighting to the fortress of Puerto Cabello, some distance away on the coast. It reported that an officer had betrayed the fortress, taking possession of it with prisoners whom he had treasonably released, and that if the General did not attack the enemy immediately from the rear, the place was lost.

Puerto Cabello was the strongest fortress on the Caribbean sea, and contained immensely precious stores of ammunition and supplies. It had been betrayed, as it was proved later, by the treachery of some of the republican officers sent with Bolívar to guard it, and Bolívar was helpless. Within a few days he, with eight loyal men, was forced to escape by ship. Bolívar was heartbroken and self-reproachful. His letter which followed his escape showed him to be crushed by the misfortune. He begged to be excused from even meeting his superior officer until he had had a few days to regain his self-control.

THE TRAGIC END

The loss of Puerto Cabello seemed to break Miranda's spirit. He was a weary man, worn with the strain of the past months and hopeless of winning victories with his present troops. He proposed an armistice, in order, as he said, to avoid the bloodshed of a long war. Terms of peace were discussed through his representatives whom he sent to meet Monteverde's men, and on July 25, 1812, he accepted them. It was his claim that he was acting only for the protection of the patriots and the future good of the cause of independence, but most of his fellow-officers were indignant at his decision to stop the fighting.

In the next few days the General finished the official business of surrender, by the terms of which the lives and property of the patriots were to be safeguarded by Monteverde. Then, as the royalist leader entered Caracas, Miranda went to the port of La Guaira. An English vessel had opportunely come into that harbor, and its captain had placed it at the General's service. He had already sent his personal papers and belongings aboard. When the captain of the ship heard that Miranda had arrived at the house of his friend Colonel Casas, the military commandant of the port, he came ashore and urged that he should return with him at once to the ship. But the General delayed for one night—and that was one night too many.

Bolívar and others of the younger patriots had been thoroughly disgusted at the surrender. They had even come to believe that Miranda was a traitor who was plotting with England, and had perhaps sold his country for his own safety or for some reward. That evening they met under Colonel Casas's roof and discussed far into the night the acts of Miranda. Hourly they became more indignant and inflamed with excitement and anger. At three o'clock in the morning they made their decision that the General was a traitor who should not be allowed to escape.

Miranda had retired to his room, utterly weary, and was sleeping with his servant outside his door. The officers, led by Bolívar, went to the room and bade the servant rouse him. At the call Miranda said, "Isn't it still very early?" He thought he was being waked to go on the ship. When he came into the room where the officers were waiting, Bolívar told him that he was their prisoner and put him under arrest. He gave up his sword and was taken secretly to the castle of San Carlos and placed in one of its dungeons.

The young men had intended to decide on their own

treatment of Miranda, but their plans went awry. Monteverde began at once to act contrary to the terms of the armistice which he had just signed. That very morning Colonel Casas received orders to close the port, and that afternoon a new commandant took over the town and gained thereby the custody of the fortress where Miranda was imprisoned.

For some months Miranda was held in one fortress and another, first in Venezuela and then in the West Indies, and at last was sent to Spain where he was thrown into a dungeon in a fortress at Cádiz. Friends worked for his release, but without avail. He remained a prisoner, chained to the wall in an underground cell, until the end of his life four years later.

Few lives have had a more tragic end. Bolívar defended his own act until his last day, declaring that Miranda was a traitor to the cause. The verdict of history is less severe. Papers have come to light which show that the surrender for which Miranda was blamed was agreed upon by the magistrates of the city and other prominent Venezuelans. He acted with them and not solely on his own judgment, as the younger patriots supposed. Those who find excuses for his decision to leave the country so quickly declare that he had made up his mind that there was no immediate hope of success with the remnants of his ill-trained army. Certainly Bolívar and his companions had no intention of letting him fall into Spanish hands, and Monteverde broke the promise of his treaty by his harsh treatment of his distinguished prisoner.

Whatever his final mistakes of judgment, Miranda had done an important service during these final years in training the young men who were to lead the more successful armies of the patriots. His assistance had been invaluable, too, in giving the new Congress courage to declare its independence and set up the First Republic of Venezuela. For thirty years he kept the cause of South American independence before the nations of the world and held exiled patriots to their high faith in his secret societies. A grateful Venezuela has done well to recognize him as the "Forerunner of Independence" and place his memorial next to that of Bolívar in its national pantheon.

We leave him with the description given by an English officer who served under him, James Briggs: "To use his own language, he abominates tyranny, hates fools, abhors flatterers, detests pride, and laments the corruption of modern days. He loves freedom, admires candor, esteems wise men, respects humility, and delights in that noble and beautiful integrity and good faith which distinguishes the golden times of antiquity. . . . He would . . . restore the ancient beatitudes, when every excellence and virtue prevailed among men, for the happiness of the present race and the perpetual prosperity of future generations."

SAN MARTÍN, SAVIOR OF THE SOUTH

THE TRAINING OF A GENERAL

*"To the two greatest men of South America—
General San Martín and myself!"*—Bolívar.

O N March 9, 1812, the British frigate *George Can-
ning* sailed into the harbor of Buenos Aires with
a quiet man of military bearing aboard whom the patriots
of that southern city were glad to see. He was Lieutenant
Colonel José San Martín, a native of Argentina, who had
been in the Spanish army for twenty-two years, and was to

be the greatest military figure of the South American Wars of Independence.

In North America we always speak of *"The* American Revolution"; for South America there are "The *Wars* of Independence." A glance at the map shows how this difference comes to be. The northern provinces of the Spanish empire, where Miranda and Bolívar began their work, were almost as remote from the southern section of the continent as if they were separate countries. The east and the west were separated, near the western coast, by the great mountain ranges of the Andes, which bounded the long, narrow territories of Peru and Chile and shut them off from the sloping plains and level, grassy pampas, which extended for hundreds of miles towards the river valleys and sea coast of the east. The wonder is not that there were separate wars, but that the "Wars of Independence" ever came to a triumphant conclusion in a final union. That climax is due to the vision and genius of two men, Simón Bolívar and José de San Martín.

The story of the freeing of the continent is like a drama, with different figures carrying on their parts in separate acts till all come together in final scenes. Two weeks and a half before the earthquake at Caracas turned the fortune of war against the patriots of Venezuela, San Martín arrived in the Plata region of the far south, where he was to be the leading figure in the next act of the great struggle for freedom. He came to a province where the first successful South American revolt against Spanish rule had already taken place.

—: 66 :—

SAN MARTÍN, SAVIOR OF THE SOUTH

HIS EARLIER YEARS
1778-1814

José Francisco de San Martín was a South American by birth, a fact which twenty-two years in the Spanish army in Europe never made him forget. He was born on February 25, 1778, in the little Indian village of Yapeyu, in the province of Misiones on Argentina's northeastern frontier. The settlement was an Indian mission planted long years before by the Jesuit fathers as a center for their work among the Guarani Indians. Today, the region is a little pocket of rich land lying between the Parana and Uruguay rivers, next door to Brazil: a region of well-watered, rolling land for the raising of cattle and semi-tropical forests, a land where oranges and lemons grow abundantly. In that beautiful country, with its luxuriant acres of grass lands and its rare flowers and birds, little José spent the first five or six years of his life, playing with the Indian children and coming to know these native people as if he were one of them by blood as well as by birth.

He was the fourth son of Juan de San Martín, who was the Spanish governor or administrator of the region. There was fighting blood on both sides of the family. The father had served in the army from his youth and was soldier in this remote region as well as governor. He had also, during his stay in Buenos Aires, been captain of a battalion of Spanish militia. His mother, Gregorio Matorias, came of pioneer stock. Her father, José's grandfather, had gained a reputation as a fighter when he led the colonists in putting down one of the revolts of the Chaco Indians.

José had his first experience of town life when his father was transferred from his inland post to Buenos Aires, but he had hardly become accustomed to the ways of this Spanish-American city when in 1785 Captain San Martín was called home to Spain. Soon young José was attending school in Madrid—a tremendous change for a seven-year-old boy who had been born in the wilds on the shores of the Uruguay river. The three older boys all went into the army, following the example of their father, and when José was eleven, he put in his request to "follow the distinguished profession of arms," and was enlisted as a cadet.

In the following years he had a good military training and much practical experience, for this was a time when there were constant wars in Europe. His first active duty, like that of Miranda, was against the Moors in Africa. Then he served in the Peninsular war under an English officer who did a good job of taking a Portuguese army and bringing it up to high standards of military efficiency. That experience was to be of use to San Martín when he set himself to train patriot armies in South America.

As the son of a Spanish officer, brought up from childhood in the army, he might well have come to feel himself as Spanish as his father. But those seven years had left their deep mark. Young San Martín made friends with other South American youth in the army and in the city when he was on leave. He heard the talk of South American independence, and went to one of the meetings of the Lautaro Society in Cádiz, which was a branch of Miranda's "Gran Reunion Americana." There were more than forty members in this group at the time when Napoleon invaded Spain, and San Martín was one of them.

THE RETURN HOME

We let him tell his own story of what followed, as he told it to friends many years later. "In 1811 I was serving in the Spanish army. Twenty years of honorable service had gained me some consideration in spite of the fact that I was an American." (He might well say so, for he had risen to the rank of lieutenant colonel for distinguished service in the Spanish campaigns against Napoleon's French armies. He had also won approval for his careful and thorough study of all the subjects, such as history, geography, and mathematics, important to his profession.) "But," he continues, "I heard of the revolution in South America; and—forsaking my fortune and my hopes—I desired only to sacrifice everything to promote the liberty of my native land."

He was a quiet young man, but he had a way of making a few warm friends. One of them could be of help to him now. He had become intimate with an Englishman, Lord Macduff, who later was to become the Earl of Fife. Through him a passport was obtained, and San Martín left Spain secretly for London. There he went to Miranda's house, where the central society still carried on its work though Miranda and Bolívar were fighting at Caracas. His two friends, Alvear and Zapiola, had come out of Spain with him, and together the three took the final pledge of devotion to the cause of South American freedom before they set sail for Buenos Aires.

There he arrived on March 9, 1812, and within eight days of his arrival he was given his rank of lieutenant colonel in the new republican army and had set about the task of organizing a squadron of "horse grenadiers," or, as we should say, cavalry. From this time on, much of his service to the patriot cause was in the training of armies. He knew, as hardly anyone else in South America knew, the value of thorough military training for soldiers. This first squadron, to which he devoted himself, became one of the most famous regiments in the southern army, supplying during the period of the wars, nineteen generals from its ranks. Other regiments modeled on it became the basis of the army which crossed the Andes.

San Martín had returned to a province which had already declared its independence from Spain. This had been done nearly two years earlier, on May 25, 1810, the great Day of Independence for Argentina, from which the republic dates its life as an independent nation. This action had followed the imprisonment of King Ferdinand VII, whom the colonists considered the rightful king. Buenos Aires had set up its own *junta,* and the viceroy had been forced to resign, leaving the control in the hands of the patriot group.

But the royalists were by no means defeated or ousted from the great Viceroyalty of La Plata, which stretched from the Atlantic westward across the broad plains and pampas to the foot of the Andes, and went far north along the three great rivers, the Parana, the Uruguay, and the Paraguay. San Martín was to spend the first two years after his return to South America with the Argentine armies in campaigns to hold the lower Plata region from royalist control or Portuguese invasion from Brazil. In one of these engagements he was wounded.

Far up towards the Andes, in Upper Peru (now Bolivia), another danger threatened the safety of the independent movement in the south. There Argentine armies under General Manuel Belgrano were endeavoring to hold back the royalist armies from across the Andes, which were due to move southward to the coast. Belgrano had won the important battle of Tucumán in 1812, and so held back the royalist advance. But that victory had been followed in 1813 by defeats. San Martín was by this time being recognized as the ablest of the Argentinean generals. He was sent, late in 1813, to this inland region, and early in 1814 he succeeded Belgrano in command of this Army of the North. It speaks well for both men that they met cordially and went on in a friendship which the changes in army rank and command did not shake.

SAN MARTÍN MAKES HIS PLAN

"The route to Peru is not here, but across the mountains to Chile."—San Martín

IN 1814, then, San Martín was in command at the spot which was considered by the men in charge of the Buenos Aires government as the test place of the war. If the Spanish forces from Peru could break through here, they could move on to take Argentina and the entire south. Here they must be held back, and from this province attacks might well be made on their stronghold in Peru.

What did San Martín do? He stayed there only a few months, studying the lay of the land, and then resigned his command. He had made up his mind that this road over the mountains was not the road to victory.

"Nothing here pleases me," he wrote to a friend. "Our country can do nothing more here than act on the defensive. . . . To think otherwise is to throw men and money into an abyss. I have already told you *my secret.*"

There must have been astonishment in Buenos Aires when the General asked to be appointed Governor of Cuyo, an Argentine province much farther to the south. There may have been suspicion, too, of his new interest in this region which was just across the mountains from Chile on the western seacoast. But there were frequent shifts of plan and changes in government in those troubled days.

What was this "secret" of San Martín's, which was soon to be anything but a secret? A look at the map of South America shows it. With the vision which only a great military leader could have had, he had seen the entire southern portion of the continent as one. He had decided that no province and no patriot government would be safe so long as the Spanish forces were entrenched in their Peruvian stronghold. Argentina could not hope for security if it defended only itself. He looked at the map as we may look at it, and drew a line from western Argentina across to Chile, and then from Chile along the Pacific Ocean northward to Peru. That was the route which must be followed. He looked at the map, but *not* as we look at it, for he knew the tremendous difficulties of that route. The Andes must be crossed, Chile must be freed, a navy must be created, and an army transported to Peru. No other man in the southern armies would have dreamed of such an undertaking, but San Martín set himself quietly and methodically to a three-year preparation.

AT MENDOZA
1814-1817

San Martín settled himself at the town of Mendoza (today, as then, the most important western town of Argentina) at the extreme western edge of the Argentine plains. It was a beautiful spot, an "inland California" in climate, as some one has said, and he must have come to it gladly, for he was far from well. The rheumatism from which he was to suffer so much in these years was already troubling him, and he had been wounded in battle in 1813. He had married soon after he landed in Buenos Aires a beautiful girl, Dona Maria Escalada, daughter of one of the leading families of the city. She was with him heart and soul in the patriot cause, staying in his camps whenever she could. Here in Mendoza it was possible for them to set up a real home.

But it was not for the beauty of the region nor for his own comfort that he had taken over the governorship of this province. He was planning to build up here a small, well-disciplined army, with which he could cross the mountains into Chile and join the patriots there. Here he was almost in the shadow of the Andes, with the great line of lofty peaks plainly visible from his camp.

We have word-portraits of San Martín all through these years. A young American, Henry Hill, who had come to South America for travel and on business, tells of meeting him in April, 1817 (after his march into Chile), at the house of his father-in-law, Signor Escalada, in Buenos Aires. He describes him in his journal as "about forty years of age, tall, dark-complexioned, with a Roman nose, and good countenance; dressed in blue, with epaulettes, and pantaloons trimmed with gold lace, and making a fine military appearance." He speaks, too, of his "eagle eye, more piercing than I had ever seen."

The real picture is of him among his people. He was a

JOSÉ FRANCISCO DE SAN MARTÍN
1778–1850
From an oil painting presented by the Argentine government
to Military Academy at West Point.

good governor. In spite of his military cares he devoted himself to the other interests of the province. Much attention was paid to education; vaccination was introduced; the public promenades were improved, and the system of irrigation was bettered. In him, says an Argentine historian, "the people saw a father whom they loved and a ruler whom they respected. His manners contributed to his authority and to the popularity gained by his deeds. His austere figure aptly symbolized the paternal despotism he established. Alone among many friends but without a confidant, he looked after everything himself, with no more help than that of one secretary and two clerks. He wore almost constantly the plain uniform of the mounted grenadiers, with the Argentine cockade on his cocked hat."

San Martín had neither the money nor the materials for the task which he had set himself, since the Argentine government was in no position to supply them even if it had seen the need of such an army or of an expedition into Chile. But gradually he won the people of Mendoza and of the entire Cuyo province to a devotion which matched his own. He began by seeking to inspire in them a spirit of patriotism. Even the children were formed into training groups, carrying their flags and doing martial exercises. He set up shops for the preparation of ammunition and supplies. A factory ran long hours for the making of army cloth, dyed blue, from which the women of Mendoza cut and sewed uniforms.

All this had been begun when there came to the help

of the General a young Franciscan monk, by the name of Fray Luis Beltran, a chaplain in the revolutionary army who was a mechanical genius with a passion for invention. The Argentine historians pile words upon words in their tales of the marvels he accomplished, and we quote one of these descriptions, that of Bartholomé Mitre, to show how everyone looked upon him—this man whom San Martín himself described as the "mainspring" of the work.

"Beltran was by intuition a mathematician, a physicist, and a chemist. As the result of observation and practice he was also an artilleryman, a maker of watches and fireworks. He was a carpenter, an architect, a blacksmith, a draughtsman, a ropemaker and a physician. He was expert in all the manual arts, and what he was ignorant of he readily acquired solely by the exercise of his extraordinary natural faculties. To all this he united a vigorous constitution, a martial bearing, and a kind and sympathetic nature."

To him the General gave, as soon as he found out his talents, the task of setting up armories for the manufacture of arms and ammunition. Here the man worked in his monk's habit. "In the midst of the noise of hammers striking anvils, and the grating of files and saws, he superintended the work of three hundred workmen, each of whom he instructed in the task assigned him. His voice was thus so affected that he remained hoarse until the end of his days."

The tale of Beltran's accomplishments runs on like a catalogue of marvels. He devised mechanical appliances

by means of which he could lower bells from their tow-
ers, and then melted them and cast the metal into cannon,
shot and shell. "He made gun-carriages, cartridges,
saddles, knapsacks, and shoes. He forged horseshoes and
bayonets and repaired damaged muskets. And with his
begrimed hand he drew on the walls of his workshop,
with a coal from the forge, designs of the contrivances by
which war material was to be transported over the dizzy
paths of the Andes."

Such enthusiasm was contagious. Everyone sought to
do his best for the cause. English foreign residents
formed a company of infantry which they placed under
San Martín's command. Landowners pastured his troop
horses free of charge, and cartmen and muleteers carried
the ammunition and supplies without cost. When word
came that an expedition of 10,000 men was due soon to
leave Spain and attack the Buenos Aires region in the
hope of crushing the patriot movement in all America,
patriotic fervor rose to the highest pitch. The ladies of
Mendoza, headed by Dona Maria San Martín, came forward to throw their jewels into the public chest. "Diamonds and pearls," they said, "are ill-suited to the present critical state of the fatherland which calls for sacrifices from all its sons. Rather than drag the chains of a
new captivity, we offer our jewels on the altar of the
fatherland."

Pleasant stories are told of San Martín at this time. A
farmer was brought before him accused of having spoken
against "La Patria." He was freed on condition that he

supply ten dozen pumpkins for the troop kitchens. An officer came in great distress to confess that he had lost in a game of chance a sum of money belonging to his regiment, money which had been entrusted to him. The governor opened a cabinet in his room, took out the needed number of gold coins, and gave them to the man, saying sternly: "Pay this money into the regimental chest, and keep the secret; for if *General* San Martín ever hears you have told of it, he will have you shot upon the spot." The officer did not tell the story until the wars were long over, and the General was living in retirement with his daughter in Paris.

AN ARMY IN TRAINING

There was a welcome and important addition to his army not long after he began his work. Chile, which had attempted a patriot government, came back into Spanish control, and a large number of patriot fugitives came over the mountains to Mendoza, there to enroll under San Martín's leadership. Among them was the Chilean army officer Bernardo O'Higgins, who had been carrying on the fight against the royalists with considerable success until a larger force came down from Peru and he was defeated in a hopeless battle when his men were outnumbered five to one. Other army men came too, but O'Higgins was the one whom San Martín chose to be his chief lieutenant during the coming months and years. The addition of the finest soldiers of the Chilean patriot army, several hundred of them according to some estimates, was a great gain for the army which was in the making. They were Chileans, eager to return to their native land and burning to right the wrongs which they and their people had suffered.

San Martín was a strict disciplinarian. The men under him had to work as they had never worked before. There were not only the long hours of drill for all the soldiers, but evening classes for the officers. After a full day's work, when their labors might well have been over, these young men studied military tactics until they knew how to handle their companies and conduct every kind of maneuver.

There was also a strong religious atmosphere in the camp. San Martín had talked much along this line with his friend General Belgrano in those months in Upper Peru. Belgrano felt, and San Martín agreed with him, that the encouragement of the native religious sentiment made for high morals in the army, as well as inspiring to patriotic self-sacrifice. Every night before taps, church prayers were said by the companies, and on Sundays the soldiers attended service and heard sermons on devotion to the fatherland, high ideals of courage, and love of liberty. The affectionate title for San Martín which has lasted down the years in the city of Mendoza is "The Saint of the Sword."

A tribute along these same lines was paid to him a couple of years later by our own Judge Breckenbridge, who came to Buenos Aires with the commissioners sent to South America by the United States government.

The great man of the country, is unquestionably San Martín. From his youth he was of a military turn of mind. . . . There are some men who possess an indescribable something which commands confidence and respect. His great application to the duties of his profession, his high character for integrity, prudence, and moral rectitude, insured him at once the esteem of the respectable among his fellow-citizens. By foreigners he was still more admired, as being more free from the vices of the creoles, and having the most enlarged and liberal views.

The standards of the time, and of Spanish-American society in South America, were not those of our northern ideas. We have to ignore and excuse much in the lives of the great leaders for freedom in these early nineteenth century days. But two South Americans stand out, conspicuous for their blameless and high-minded personal lives. One is San Martín; the other Antonio Sucre, who was the right-hand man of Simón Bolívar in his later campaigns—Sucre, the victor of the Battle of Ayacucho, the final battle of the Wars of Independence.

THE MARCH ACROSS THE ANDES

One of the four great mountain marches of all history

FROM Mendoza San Martín looked out for three years on the range of snow-capped Andes which separated the Argentine pampas from the beautiful valleys of Chile. "What spoils my sleep," he said at this time, "is not the strength of the enemy, but how to pass those immense mountains."

There were passes by which they could be crossed at the height of the summer season (which was in January, for below the equator the seasons are the opposite of those on our northern continent), but such crossings were usually made by small parties of merchants or soldiers who were often forced by the narrowness of the path to proceed in single file. Our young American business man, Mr. Hill, who made the crossing at about this time, gives a vivid account of it. "The rocky mountainsides," he says, "rise from the river almost perpendicularly several hundred feet, with the narrow path of shelf having been made by scooping out or excavating the rock almost on the edge of the precipice." "The path," he continues, "is from one to two feet in width, just sufficient for the mule to pass. Looking up, the mountain top is in the clouds. The precipice below is a look of horror. You look down a gulf of five hundred feet (and in one place seven hundred descent), at the bottom of which rolls the furious Mendoza river."

"TO THE FIRST SHOT"

Such were the passes, all of them from nine thousand to twelve thousand feet above sea level, over which San Martín proposed to transport an army with all its necessary equipment. It was no wonder that the feat was considered impossible. Yet in November of 1815, when the Spanish cause was triumphing everywhere in South America, with the patriots in one region and another suffering defeat, the General rose to his feet at the close of a banquet to which he had invited his officers and proposed a toast: "To the first shot fired beyond the Andes against the oppressors of Chile!"

This seems to have been the first open and public acknowledgment of San Martín's purpose. He made it at a moment of great gloom among all patriots. The Spaniards had just routed completely an army in Upper Peru, winning the victory at Sipe-Sipe, a victory which, according to one Spanish historian of the time, "beheaded the revolution." In Europe, King Ferdinand VII, lately restored to his throne, was being congratulated by his fellow monarchs on the re-conquest of South America which was considered to be practically accomplished.

Then it was that San Martín decided that he should make his plan known. That toast, "To the first shot fired beyond the Andes—," was his dramatic notice to the world

ACROSS THE ANDES

"What spoils my sleep is how to pass those immense mountains."—
San Martin

that the South American cause was not dead, nor dying. His officers responded with a cheer. Confidence came back to them with a rush. From that hour they were committed heart and soul to the undertaking.

Outside of Cuyo, the plan, when it was reported, was considered by the military men of the United Provinces of Argentina to be utterly impracticable and foolhardy. The route across the Uspallata Pass (at the summit of which there stands today the famous statue of the Christ of the Andes, marking the boundary between Argentina and Chile) was not unused. Travelers and traders went back and forth along it. The conquistadores had found it out when they were exploring the southern part of the continent. Small companies of Chilean and Argentine soldiers had gone back and forth during the opening days of the Wars of Independence. But the idea of taking a large army over this mountain barrier had never occurred to anyone. It is said that when the great march was over and the Spaniards met the San Martín army at Chacabuco, their surprise was not only at the number of men who had made the crossing but at their perfect equipment. They *could* imagine men making the march, though hardly in any such numbers, but they had counted on any companies who came being so poorly equipped for battle that they could be easily overcome.

San Martín had studied those mountain ranges as they had never been studied before. He had had his engineers reconnoitering all along the long stretch of the Cordilleras so that every pass was known. Moreover, he had set up a spy system by which he was kept informed of every move made in Chile, while he managed by spreading false rumors to keep the enemy completely misinformed about his own plans. Letters were sent out in the fall of 1816 which he intended to have fall into the hands of the Spanish authorities, indicating that he intended to send his main army across by the passes of the south, whereas his real purpose was to go over the mountains at a point much farther north.

He even went so far as to invite to a conference at Mendoza a tribe of southern Indians who lived across the mountains along the eastern slopes. To tempt them into coming, he sent along with his invitation mules laden with gifts; and they came in all their savage pomp, bringing their women with them and staging a sham battle for his benefit when they arrived. The General told the Indians that the Spaniards were foreigners who would rob them of their lands and cattle, and they listened and gave him permission to bring his army over their mountain passes and through their territory, which was far to the south. The result of all this campaign of talk was that the Captain-General of Chile, the Spanish commander, tried to spread his defense southward as well as northward along the whole lengthy front of the east slopes of the Andes, with no idea at what point the expected attack might come. And we must remember that Chile is a narrow ribbon of land stretching hundreds upon hundreds of miles along the Pacific coast.

As the time drew near the preparations at Mendoza

were pushed to completion. Nothing had been left undone that could be done. Special carriages had been designed and built for the transportation of the artillery over the mountain passes. Slings were prepared for swinging the guns on the backs of mules. The comfort and sustenance of the soldiers had been considered. They were to make their marches through regions where there was little or no food. A special food had been made up of beef which had been dried and ground to powder, mixed with fat and Chile pepper, and pounded into small cakes. A soldier could carry in his knapsack a supply which would feed him for eight days. For the crossing of ravines where there was no safe bridge, a strong portable bridge of four cables, not unlike those of the Incas of long ago, was constructed. There was no detail of equipment or preparation which was too small for San Martín's personal attention.

THE DEDICATION

When the hour of departure was drawing near, San Martín set apart a day for the dedication of the army. He knew the value among his people of a dramatic occasion as well as did his northern counterpart, Bolívar. But San Martín's occasions never centered around himself or his own leadership, while Bolívar used effectively and successfully his personal charm and power to gain his results by the enthusiasm of his followers.

That day the entire army of four thousand men marched from its camps to the city of Mendoza, which was prepared for the festival with flower-covered arches,

banners, and lines of floating streamers and hangings. The
bells of the eight churches pealed a welcome as the soldiers
formed in the great central plaza. General Belgrano had
doubtless told San Martín of his own triumph following
the battle of Tucumán, when the statue of Our Lady of
Mercy was being carried in procession through the streets
as part of the celebration of her holy day, on which the
victory had been won. Meeting the procession, Belgrano
had gone forward reverently and placed his baton in the
hand of the statue, while the people gave thanks for their
escape and victory. Now San Martín carried out a similar
ceremonial in the cathedral, in the presence of a great company of officials and citizens. The banner of the army,
which had been embroidered by the ladies of Mendoza
and ornamented with rich jewels, was prayed over and
blessed, and with it the General's own baton. This baton
he placed in the statue's hand, and then he took the banner and went out to a platform which had been built in
the square before the cathedral. The troops were waiting
there. As the General faced them, they presented arms,
while the drums beat a march of honor. Then in the
silence which followed, he held up the beautiful banner
before them for all to see.

"Soldiers!" he said in a deep voice which carried to the
farthest corner of the plaza, "this is the first banner of independence which has been blessed in America."

As he waved it before them three times, the soldiers and
people responded with a loud shout of "Vivá la Patria!
Long live the Fatherland!"

Again the General, who stood with head uncovered, spoke. "Soldiers! Swear, as I do, to uphold it and die in its defense."

"We swear," the answer rolled back from the great multitude as if it were spoken by a single voice.

A discharge of musketry and a salute of twenty-five guns completed the ceremony. The "March Across the Andes" had become a patriotic crusade, like the crusades of the Middle Ages.

ACHIEVEMENT

The word to start was given in early January. Day after day the divisions moved out, each to its appointed road and towards its appointed place of attack. The first detachment went over a northern pass to occupy a friendly region where the patriots were fairly strong and there was only a small royalist force. When that province was occupied, they could move down and reinforce their brothers to the south. Other divisions moved off on the dates set. The plan had been worked out by San Martín and his staff six or seven months earlier. If we did not know from other travelers of the difficulties of those mountain passes, the reports of the various movements of the troops would sound like the record of army maneuvers on level ground. But there are hints, too, of hardships and suffering from the terrific climbs and from the mountain sickness which attacked the men as they came up into the clouds. The highest point of one of these passes over which the troops moved is nearly thirteen thousand feet, a mile higher than some of the famous passes over the Alps in Switzerland. Many of the animals perished on the journey, but the men did not falter.

Like clockwork the plan was worked out. On the given date the entire army of four thousand men with its ammunition and equipment was at its appointed posts in Chile. The distance from Mendoza to the battlefield of Chacabuco where the great battle was soon to be fought was three hundred miles by one of the routes taken, and more than that by another. The series of marches spread the troops over a front of thirteen hundred miles in Chile.

Of course these troops under San Martín and O'Higgins won their famous victory on the plains of Chacabuco a few days later. How could Spanish troops sent from a distance on a mere routine errand of defending a province hold their own against these crusaders, these men who had been living and working for months with a single goal in mind, and who had triumphed over the tremendous barrier of one of the highest mountain ranges of the continent?

The "March Across the Andes" stands out in the military history of the world. Two other famous marches, both over the Alps, are ranked with it: that of Hannibal and his army in ancient times over the pass of Little St. Bernard, and that of Napoleon and his troops over the Great St. Bernard pass into Italy. But historians agree that this march of San Martín was in many ways the greatest feat. The passes through which his marching armies had to make their way were higher than the Alpine passes,

SAN MARTÍN AND O'HIGGINS CROSSING THE MOUNTAINS

and the valleys through which at least two of the divisions of the army had to move were arid desert, uninhabited and offering no support for his troops. A fourth spectacular march was to be added to the list two years later when Bolívar made his famous crossing of the Andes on the line of the equator. But that was a venture showing human daring and endurance, with terrific sacrifice of human life. San Martín's success was due in large measure to his long and thorough preparation. It stands in history as a monument to his genius, never to be forgotten so long as men journey across that lofty mountain range.

SAN MARTÍN IN CHILE

"Chile must first be freed from her oppressors."—San Martín

SIX months before the crossing of the Andes, General San Martín had selected the spot where he and his army would choose to do battle with the Spaniards, near the gorge of Chacabuco by the junction of two rivers, the Aconcagua and the Putaendo. Here the two armies met, and one of the important and decisive battles of the Wars of Independence was fought. The royalists were surprised and defeated, with the loss of twelve hundred of their best men. The tale of the battle is a matter of military history long past. It is with the result of these battles that we are concerned. This battle of Chacabuco, fought on February 12, 1817, was important because it scattered the Spanish forces in the northern part of Chile and opened the door to the Chilean capital, Santiago. Two days after it was fought San Martín and his able lieutenant, the Chilean O'Higgins, entered the city.

There was no great enthusiasm in Santiago over the coming of the Argentine general with his army. Chile had an old Spanish civilization, which had been built up during three hundred years, and the patriot cause was not popular with the wealthier ruling families. The conservative landowners, and the business men who owned and managed the mines and carried on a busy seacoast trade, might desire political independence from a distant Spain which was breaking up through foreign invasion; but they did not wish to have their own old order of life upset by a group of revolutionaries.

There are interesting bits of history along the way which surprise us. When San Martín and O'Higgins entered Santiago after the victory of Chacabuco, the assembly, which had taken over the government on the flight to the north of the Spanish higher officials, offered San Martín the headship of the government. He declined, suggesting that the position be given to his Chilean associate, O'Higgins, who had won distinction in the "March Across the Andes" and the recent battle. They then voted him ten thousand ounces of gold for the expenses of his journey—this, for that amazing mountain march of his rescue army! And what did he do with it? There was never a moment in all these years when San Martín did not need money for his plans and need it desperately. He had declined the Chilean honors because he was too busy with his project of freeing Peru. But he promptly devoted that sum of gold to the establishment of a public library in Santiago. Again and again we see these patriot leaders stop between battles to do some such act which would help towards the future of the common people. They were forced for the time being to make war, but they were always looking towards peace and a new South America.

Chile was not won by a single battle, nor did the naming of O'Higgins as Director bring peace between factions that had been torn by civil war. The central part of the country was in patriot hands, but two strong fortresses, Talcahuano and Valdivia, in southern Chile remained in the possession of the Spaniards, who could send in reinforcements from the sea to hold this whole section of the narrow country. San Martín stayed in Chile only a short time after the entrance into Santiago. He knew that Chile would never be safe until it had control of the sea, and such control could never be complete without the freeing of Peru. It was his duty to leave Chilean affairs for the time being in other hands and hurry back over those mountain passes and across the broad pampas of Argentina to Buenos Aires, there to report his success and gain support for his next project. It is characteristic of the man that he managed to get to Buenos Aires a day earlier than he was expected and so avoided the demonstrations which had been planned in honor of his victorious homecoming.

Again, as in the case of the work at Mendoza, the General seems to have had to take almost the entire burden on his own shoulders. The Argentine leaders were willing to coöperate in the creation of a fleet on the Pacific Ocean, *provided* the Chileans agreed (as San Martín promised for them) to make a large contribution towards that fleet and towards the maintenance of the Argentine army in Upper Peru. The Chileans must also pay for the support of the Army of the Andes now stationed with them. San Martín returned to Chile with these promises, and a representative of the Argentine government soon followed to confirm them. If all these plans could have been carried out at once, much suffering might have been avoided. But the patriot governments were unstable. There was strife among the leaders in Buenos Aires, and when San Martín came back to Chile he found that O'Higgins was hard put to it to maintain his authority. His power was considered by the Chileans to rest too much on the support of the foreign army which he and San Martín had brought over from Mendoza.

THE BATTLE OF MAIPÚ

The Spaniards took advantage of the delay to act. Four shiploads of soldiers, thirty-four hundred trained men with a supply of two hundred and thirty cannon and full equipment for a campaign, came to southern Chile in January, 1818. O'Higgins did what he could to gather his forces, but in March the patriot forces under himself and San Martín met defeat. Rumors came to the capital after that engagement that San Martín had been killed and O'Higgins wounded to the death. The Chilean royalists in Santiago were already celebrating and preparing to take over the government when O'Higgins rode into the city, and the confusion ended. Next came word that San Martín was alive, with an army of four thousand men reassembled, and shortly he, too, rode into the city.

It was then that the General made what is said to be the one and only public speech of his life. He was utterly worn by hard riding and loss of sleep following the battle, but as he reined up at his house and dismounted from his horse, he turned and spoke to the rejoicing crowd which had assembled on the news of his safety. In a few quick sentences he assured all those within hearing of his voice that he expected to win the next battle, and to win it soon.

On April 5, 1818, he made good that promise. He had re-created an army from all the scattered divisions. Now he met the large royalist army at Maipú, a few miles south-west of Santiago, on a line of low hills. It was from one of these hills that he looked out that day at dawn on a cloudless sky and remarked to his officers, "I take the sun to witness that the day is ours"; and from another vantage point, after the battle had been raging for some time, that he surveyed the fighting of the different divisions and said, "The fate of Chile will be decided in half an hour." It *was* so decided, and for the patriots. Maipú was one of the hardést fought battles of the Wars of Independence, with a large number of men engaged on each side. The victory ended the Spanish power in Chile, save for a few northern points which were soon taken by sea attack.

AMONG THE CHILEANS

Nearly two years were to pass, even after this victory, before San Martín could carry out his plan and move on Peru. Before we go on to that story we get one or two glimpses of his personal life in these years. The hardships which he had endured began to affect his health seriously. His rheumatism was so crippling at one time that he had to be carried across the mountains on a litter.

Yet he persisted in these transcontinental trips which would be considered today a strenuous exploit for a hardy mountaineer. At one time we hear of his spending a few weeks at a town where there were mineral springs, taking the baths in an effort to regain his freedom and comfort in movement.

Yet while we are hearing these reports, there comes another picture, again from young Henry Hill, who was by this time establishing a mercantile house in Santiago and was made United States consul in 1818. He writes that the General "had a weekly *soirée* at his residence where the *élite* of Santiago assembled." These gatherings, he says, tended greatly to increase the patriotic spirit. "Before separating, and when all were standing, the thrilling and inspiriting national song, 'Hear, O Mortals, the sacred shouts,' was sung by the entire group, accompanied by his fine military band, and with an ardor and enthusiasm almost enchanting. Often have I seen him on his daily horseback rides to drill and care for his black regiment, to whom he was strongly attached."

One more impression of him can be given at this time, although its date is a little later. Captain Basil Hall, the English traveler, describes him as a "man of stalwart frame, with a fiery spirit hidden under a studious reserve of manner, which at times exploded." His appearance, he says, was that of the soldier. He carried his head very erect, and his chin and jaw showed strength of will. His thick black hair he wore cut short above his straight, high forehead. His large black eyes were overhung by heavy

eyebrows which met when he frowned. It is the portrait
of a stern man. One can see why the pleasure-loving
Chilean society folk did not fall under his spell as his
soldiers did. But Captain Hall adds, from the experience
of his own visit with him, that the General was "thoroughly well-bred and unaffectedly simple in his manners,
exceedingly cordial and engaging, and possessed evidently
of great kindliness of disposition."

ON TO PERU

*"Four ships gave the western continent to Spain;
these four will take it from her."*—O'Higgins

So spoke O'Higgins, "Supreme Director of Chile,"
hopefully, defiantly, in October, 1818, as he stood
on a high hill outside of the city of Santiago and watched
four little vessels spreading their sails to a fresh south-
west breeze far out on the Pacific.

In his secret heart O'Higgins doubtless knew that four
ships could not end the dominion of Spain. Victory was
not to be so easy as that. But he had been brought by San
Martín to know that the patriot cause could never gain
permanent security so long as the stronghold of Spanish
rule, Peru, remained unconquered. And Peru could not
be taken so long as a Spanish fleet could range the waters
of the Pacific for its protection. Those four ships which
were sailing proudly out to sea with the Chilean flag at
their mastheads were the beginning of a patriot navy on
the Pacific.

When San Martín began to make his plans for the freeing of Peru, the sea must have looked almost as much of a
barrier as had the high Andean mountains. Nor was San
Martín a sea-going man. His experience did not lie along
those lines. But he knew that there must be a navy, and

sent his agents to buy ships in English and American ports with such money as he was able to obtain from the Chilean and Buenos Aires governments. Those four little ships over which O'Higgins was gloating in the fall of 1818 were the beginning of that navy.

It was such a tiny fleet—just four vessels which had been picked up by the patriots within the few months since the freeing of Chile. One was an English ship purchased for San Martín in London and only recently arrived. Another was an East India company frigate. It had been purchased by a loan from a group of Chilean merchants, with the additional help of a guarantee of ten thousand dollars from the Argentine government. The other two were American, a brig and a privateer. They had, amongst them, one hundred and forty-two mounted guns, while the Pacific fleet of the Spaniards had three hundred and thirty guns on its seventeen vessels. But the Chilean vessels were commanded by able English and American officers, who had come gladly into this service, and there were eleven hundred Chilean sailors and soldiers aboard. They had been renamed, too, with patriot names, the *San Martín,* the *Lautaro,* the *Aracauno,* and the *Chacabuco.* Director O'Higgins had a right to be proud of them, knowing the joy they would bring to General San Martín when he returned from Buenos Aires.

A new figure appeared on the scene at this time, an Englishman who was a godsend to San Martín and the patriot cause. He was Lord Thomas Cochrane, a capable and experienced military officer, who had left the British

Isles because he was under some kind of a cloud there, and came out to offer his services in the fight against Spain. He took over and built up the little Chilean fleet, training its men for the quick expeditions and sudden attacks by which he was to distinguish himself here. With him as admiral, San Martín and O'Higgins were able to complete the patriot conquest of Chile, for he captured from the water the northern seaport forts to which the last of the Spanish forces finally retreated.

It was well that there was something to give cheer on the Pacific coast, for on the Atlantic things were going badly, as San Martín discovered on his visits to Buenos Aires. There was fear there of attack from abroad. King Ferdinand VII, newly restored to his throne, threatened to send a huge expedition across the Atlantic to bring his rebellious colonists into line; and the Argentineans, under that threat, did not want to spend money on a distant expedition. There was civil strife, too, between the different leaders and provinces in Argentina, and in the end San Martín had to move out without the support of his home government. A lesser man would have given up the effort, but not San Martín. He was convinced that no colony would be safe until the Spanish stronghold in Peru was taken, and on that conviction he acted, in spite of the lack of enthusiasm in both Argentina and Chile.

"Whatever be my lot in the campaign in Peru," he announced in reply to his critics, "I shall prove that ever since I returned to my native land, independence has occupied my every thought."

In 1820 Admiral Cochrane told San Martín that he had cleared the Pacific waters so that he could transport an army to any point desired. The General was ready with his troops, and on a September day, the line of ships dropped anchor in a harbor one hundred and fifty miles south of Lima, Peru's capital city, and forty-five hundred patriot soldiers, Argentineans and Chileans, went ashore. San Martín had accomplished the next step in his program for independence. He had freed Chile. Now he had achieved what had been thought impossible. By his newly created navy he had brought an army to the doors of the stronghold of Spanish power on the continent.

AS "PROTECTOR OF PERU"
1821-1822

The manner of General San Martín's freeing of Peru is as unusual as the spirit of the man who planned it. "Remember," he told his soldiers as they landed in the southern section of the country, "that you are come, not to conquer, but to liberate a people. The Peruvians are our brothers."

His opening campaign was both political and military. He knew that there was a strong group of patriots in the city of Lima, and that there were patriot sympathizers in every town. His army was too small for a quick conquest. He could not make a direct and immediate attack on the capital. But he counted on the Peruvians to join with him, and they did. Daily his numbers grew as men came into his camp from all over the country. Gradually, in a series of slow movements, he encircled Lima, approaching it with a small army from the south while he took the larger force northward by sea and then came back by land, shutting the city in. Meanwhile Admiral Cochrane did his part brilliantly by sea.

It took patience to play such a waiting game, but the General knew what he was doing, for he was in touch with the political leaders within the city. One Spanish viceroy resigned, and was succeeded by another, chosen from among the Spanish generals. In time he, too, came to know that he was beaten, for the city was being starved out. He withdrew, as San Martín had expected he would, to the inland plateaux, and the news of that withdrawal came to the General's camp. It was amazing news. The capital of Peru, the three-hundred-year-old city of Pizarro's founding, had been evacuated by its Spanish rulers and come into the General's possession without any attack being made on it.

History is filled with pictures of dramatic entries into cities by conquering generals. But there is no other like this entry of San Martín into Lima. He did not even hasten to take possession, but waited until a *cabildo,* a governing group of Peruvian citizens, invited him to enter. Then, on July 21, 1821, he rode quietly into the city, accompanied by only a single aide-de-camp, and went to the palace of the viceroys. At the news of his coming the citizens came together joyfully to welcome him. Bolívar would have made a great demonstration on such on occasion, but San Martín had no interest in such personal triumphs. He received the officials politely, but the story is that he was so wearied by their extreme gratitude and desire to do him honor that he slipped out of the city again that night to sleep in his quarters in a neighboring village. A week later at the celebration of the birth of the new republic, a young priest in the crowd raised the shout of "Vivá San Martín!", but the General said quickly, "Do not say that. Say rather, 'Vivá la independencia del Perú!'"

We are fortunate in having a report of an interview with General San Martín at this time. The English traveler, Captain Basil Hall, went on board his ship and talked long with him. The report of the conversation shows that this conquest was different from any of the other enterprises of the Wars of Independence. It shows, too, that at this time San Martín reached greater heights in his devotion to the principles of freedom than any other leader of his time.

"The contest in Peru," he told the Englishman, "is not a war of conquest and glory, but of opinion. It is a war of new and liberal principles against prejudice, bigotry, and tyranny. People ask why I don't march into Lima at once. So I might, and instantly would, were it suitable to my views, which it is not. I do not want military renown; I have no ambition to be conqueror of Peru. I want solely to liberate the country from oppression."

He went further, with views that are as modern as the twentieth century and might well be heeded by its dictators. "I wish," he said, "to have all men thinking with me, and do not choose to advance a step beyond the march of public opinion. . . . Public opinion is an engine newly introduced into this country. The Spaniards, who are utterly incapable of directing it, have prohibited its use; but they shall now experience its strength and importance."

On another day he said to the Englishman: "All I wish is that this country should be managed by itself, and by itself alone. As to the manner in which it is to be governed, that belongs not at all to me. I propose simply to give the people the means of declaring themselves independent, and of establishing a suitable form of government; after which I shall consider I have done enough and leave them."

If only it could have worked out as simply and clearly as that! But the story cannot be ended there. San Martín was to find it necessary to take soon the title of "Protector of Peru," and to govern until the people should be able to carry on their own government. The royalists were by no means driven out or defeated in the southern part of the country or in the mountains to which they retired. There were jealousies and criticisms by Peruvian officials and army men. San Martín was not popular with the common people or with the society folk of Lima. They accused him of being too stern and of keeping too much power in his own hands, as a military man would be likely to do. In the end, Bolívar was to come in by San Martín's invitation and finish the task. But in San Martín's mind this use of his authority seems to have been only during the emergency. In his farewell address in 1822 he said to the people that he was tired of hearing them say that he wanted to be king. His true desire was for public opinion to assert itself and rule, and he had written his personal wish to his friend O'Higgins in 1821:

"At last, by patience, we have compelled the enemy to abandon the capital of the Pizarros. . . . I now see before me the end of my public life, and watch how I can leave this heavy charge in safe hands, so that I may retire into some quiet corner and live as a man should live."

This was the true San Martín, but these words were written a year before the unhappy meeting with Bolívar.

THE MEETING WITH BOLÍVAR

It is easy from a safe distance in time to tell what men should have done in the face of difficulties. Looking back we can say that San Martín should have proceeded more rapidly with his military movements. But he was on the spot and knew conditions, as we do not. The country was a difficult one to occupy, with its deserts and river valleys, its high inland plateaux behind the mountain ranges. As the months passed, San Martín came to know that his own forces were too weak to drive the royalists wholly out of the country. He despaired of getting help from the distant government at Buenos Aires or from Chile, and turned to the Liberator, Bolívar, who was coming down with his forces from the north. If they two could make a union, and Bolívar could supply him troops, the final victory would come more quickly.

Early in the year 1822 he wrote to Bolívar, and in July he went north to a borderland region, between Peru and the northern part of Quito (now Ecuador) to meet him. The meeting was unfortunate from the start. Bolívar had arrived at this harbor of Guayaquil a fortnight before he had been expected, and received the southern general as if he were a guest on Colombian territory. From the moment of his arrival San Martín knew that he had lost all chance of discussing the control of this borderland region with Bolívar. "The Liberator has been too quick for us," he remarked to a friend on board his ship.

San Martín had come to the conference with high hopes. "We shall see each other," he had written to Bolívar, "and I forecast that America will not forget the day we embrace." The first day Bolívar gave a reception in the General's honor. A banquet followed, and then the two retired and conversed for an hour and a half. The next day there was a brief call of ceremony by San Martín, but he was already ordering his baggage sent to the schooner. It was plain that things were not going well. Before the final ball that evening there was a long conference, and soon after midnight the General departed.

For a time no one knew what was discussed. Now we know that the two men exchanged views on the future of the colonies and disagreed. San Martín had seen so much of the difficulties of republican government in Buenos Aires, Chile and Peru, that he felt that a ruler should take charge until the people should gain experience, and suggested the idea, quite common in South America in those

days, of such a ruler from one of the royal families of
Europe. Bolívar disagreed sharply. He believed in a great
confederation of all the South American territories under
one general republican leader.

The serious disagreement came, however, on the conduct of the war. San Martín asked for soldiers, saying
that with three or four thousand more, he could finish the
war in three months. Bolívar hesitated until at last the
General felt that the question might be one of command,
and offered to put himself under Bolívar if enough troops
could be sent with the Liberator in command. It was a
remarkably unselfish offer, but Bolívar did not accept it.
He said politely that he could not think of allowing the
Argentine leader to humble himself in that way. San
Martín came to feel that the only way to get Bolívar's
help for Peru was for him to withdraw.

The interviews ended, and the two men sat down together at the banquet. At that dinner Bolívar gave his
toast, "To the two greatest men in South America, General San Martín and myself!" San Martín's toast in reply
was, "To the speedy conclusion of the war; to the organization of the different Republics of the Continent; to the
health of the Liberator of Colombia!"

President Bolívar thoroughly enjoyed the ball which
followed, as he always enjoyed such festivities. General
San Martín, never fond of such occasions, found this one
more than he could bear, in the face of his bitter disappointment. At 1 A.M. he called his aide and said to him,
"Let us go. I cannot stand this riot." Bolívar accompanied

Courtesy Pan-American Union

MONUMENT TO THE ARMY OF THE ANDES

him in the darkness to the dock and bade him farewell. When San Martín landed in Peru, he found that there was trouble among his officials, who were disputing his authority. He called a Congress and resigned as "Protector of Peru." He gave his health as one reason for his departure, and he scolded the Peruvians a little. "I am tired," he told them, "of hearing them call me a tyrant, that I wish to make myself King, Emperor, the Devil. On the other hand, my health is broken, this climate is killing me. I think I have now the right to dispose of my old age." But to a single friend he wrote frankly: "There is not room in Peru for both Bolívar and myself. . . . Let him enter, that America may triumph."

DEPARTURE

The rest of the story is quickly told. San Martín slipped away from Lima in the darkness of night almost as if he were a fugitive instead of its deliverer, and took ship for Chile. There he lay ill, seriously ill, for a couple of months. In February of 1823, he made another crossing of the Andes, this one to be his last. He had hoped to settle for a time in Mendoza, but there came to him there the news of his wife's death in Buenos Aires. Towards the close of that year he took his only child, his daughter Mercedes, and sailed for Europe.

There he lived for another twenty-seven years, spending his last days in a house near Paris given him by a banker friend of his soldier years in the Spanish army, who found him in poverty and insisted on making him comfortable. From this "loophole of retreat," as he called it, he could look out on the world, reading much and following with keen interest events in his native land.

San Martín died in 1850, apparently forgotten by the land for which he had done so much. But later generations began to do him honor. His remains were brought back from Europe to be deposited in the beautiful cathedral of Buenos Aires, and his memory has grown in honor through the years. He is recognized by historians as one of the greatest military leaders of all time, but South America remembers him more for his great vision, and his utter and unselfish devotion in carrying it out. He described himself once when he wrote that he had "ceased to belong to himself, but belonged rather to the cause of the American continent."

FOUR HEROES OF THE SOUTH

MORENO
ARTIGAS
BELGRANO
O'HIGGINS

MORENO, CHAMPION OF FREE SPEECH

"He was the soul of the revolution of 1810"

MARIANO MORENO worked actively in the revolution in Argentina for less than two years, and at its very beginning. His first public paper was a written protest, not even signed by his name, which was handed to the Spanish viceroy at Buenos Aires on September 30, 1809. He died at sea on his way to England as a delegate of the *junta* in March, 1811. Yet in that short period he proved that the pen is at least as powerful as the sword, if not far more so. He left in those few months his own personal stamp on the whole southern movement for independence.

ADVOCATE OF NATIONAL INDEPENDENCE

America was a long way from Europe at the beginning of the nineteenth century, when the voyage between the two continents took long weeks which ran into months. Yet the destiny of South America was profoundly affected by every move in the capitals of France, Portugal, and Spain.

To each colony came the news of Napoleon's victories; of his invasion of Spain, and of the imprisonment of Ferdinand VII, the lawful heir to the throne, while Joseph Bonaparte was put in his place. In Caracas, far to the north, young Venezuelan patriots—among them, Simón Bolívar—stormed the palace of the viceroy when the news came, and sent the French envoys who had been its bearers scurrying to their ships for safety. They would have no dealings with a French ruler. In the Plata colonies in the south, other young men saw their opportunity and took steps at once for South American independence. One of these young leaders was Mariano Moreno, another, Manuelo Belgrano. Argentina remembers both with pride.

One feels that we of today would have liked Mariano Moreno and had more in common with him than with some of the more fiery orators and political figures of those days. He believed in the things we believe in and went about the business of getting them in our kind of way, a way that we like to call "American." When the patriot *junta* took over the government from the viceroy, he presented at its councils a resolution for the immediate publication of a weekly newspaper which should be a publicity sheet for the new government with open columns for the expression of opinions by private individuals. Of this journal, the *Gaceta de Buenos Aires,* he became the editor. In its third issue he wrote an article pleading for freedom of thought and speech which is so modern in its ideas that it might as well have been published in Boston or New York in 1930 or 1940 as in Buenos Aires on June 21, 1810, except for the more stilted language.

The people, he said, must throw away their "antiquated opinions" or they would stay in a "shameful state of stupefaction" in which there could be no advance in arts or in useful knowledge. Truth, he declared, like virtue, "contains within itself its most convincing apology"; discussion and examination cause the "splendor and luster" of both to become fully apparent. "If restrictions are placed upon speech, the spirit of man will vegetate as does matter: error, falsehood, prejudice, fanaticism, and stupefaction will become the devices of the people, and will cause their perpetual decadence, ruin, and misery." Wise words, these, for any time!

HIS EDUCATION

Born in Buenos Aires in 1778, Mariano Moreno had the best education which South America could offer, and that was saying a great deal in those opening years of the nineteenth century. When the Spanish aristocrats and cultured church fathers found themselves, in the seventeenth and eighteenth centuries, exiled by their duties in the wealth-bringing American colonies, they founded schools and universities for their sons. They were determined to set up a social and intellectual life as nearly as possible like that of the homeland.

Young Moreno attended the best schools in Buenos Aires, and then went on to the local College of San Carlos, where he won distinction as a scholar. He was not willing to stop there, but took the long, difficult overland journey into the mountains of Upper Peru (now Bolivia), there to study letters, theology, and law at the famous University of San Francisco Javier. On his return he was soon drawn into the efforts for freedom, of which he was to be the able spokesman.

IN BUENOS AIRES

Two years before Moreno was born, Spain had recognized the growing importance of this region in the east and south by setting up a great Viceroyalty of La Plata which took in the entire eastern section of the continent, south of Brazil, reaching to the base of the mountains which separated it from Chile. Hitherto the Plata valley had been looked upon chiefly as the Atlantic outlet for the thoroughfare across the continent to Peru. As a viceroyalty this territory gained the privilege of trading directly with Spain, instead of carrying on its trade through the officials of Peru; and thus Buenos Aires came to be an important commercial center.

Moreno had hardly settled himself in the city when the trouble in Europe began. The first effect was an English invasion, which gave Moreno his first and only taste of soldiering and furthered the spirit of independence in the colony. England, considering herself at war with the Spain of Napoleonic rule, decided to make an attempt to gain a much desired foothold on the Atlantic coast. British ships attacked both Buenos Aires and Montevideo, the city on the other side of the wide Plata river, expecting apparently to get some support from the discontented colonists. Instead, there was a hastily organized defense, and the English were driven out of the country. The importance of this episode was the sense of independence which the colonists gained. The Spanish authorities had done little. The Argentineans had had to act by themselves in the defense of their country. They acquired a sense of their own power which was not forgotten when the next occasion arose.

The tale of the Argentine Revolution runs according to a pattern familiar to us of the United States. The wealthy colonists were driven for years to the brink of rebellion by annoying and unreasonable restrictions on their trade and by excessive taxes. When the new viceroy came out from Spain in July, 1809, the Argentineans handed him a long "memorial" of protest written by their lawyer-patriot, Moreno. It was just such a paper as the colonists of the North American seaports had presented to the British authorities before the American Revolution. Moreover, it contained a stern reminder that such oppression by England in the colonies of the northern continent had led them to turn against the mother country.

This viceroy came from the Spanish Regency, which was acting for the imprisoned king. He should have been wise enough to heed this warning, but he did not, except to make a few small concessions. On May fifteenth of the following year, when he got the news that French soldiers were sweeping across Spain, he was so foolish as to issue a proclamation admitting that fact but boasting that even if the home country was conquered, the "liberty and independence of the Spanish monarchy would be preserved within the confines of the American continent." Though defeated at home, Spain would rule its colonies.

The patriots thought otherwise. They forced the viceroy to summon an "open council," which was the only chance the people had, under the Spanish system, for an expression of popular opinion. The council met and decided after long discussion, which was led by Moreno, Belgrano, and others, to take over the viceroy's powers. Within a couple of days a *junta* of nine members was appointed of which Moreno was secretary.

Then came May 25, 1810, the great Day of Independence for Argentina, from which the republic dates its life as an independent nation. On that morning the *junta* met to receive the resignation of the viceroy, who proved to be the last Spanish official ever to rule over the Plata provinces. A great crowd thronged the central plaza of the town and shouted with joy as the blue and white colors of the patriot flags swung out in the breeze, and the news was given that the final act of separation had been performed. Within the hall, the members of the *junta,* with Moreno and Belgrano among them, were acknowledging the imprisoned Ferdinand as their king, but in spite of these words they were giving no allegiance to the ruling *junta* government in Spain. In other words, they were setting up self-government, with no allegiance to any active government overseas. The pledge to the imprisoned king became, therefore, only a form of words so far as the real control of their own affairs was concerned. Today the finest avenue in the splendid city of Buenos Aires is called the *Avenida de Mayo* (Avenue of May) in honor of that day and the patriot group of founders of the republic.

AS EDITOR AND PUBLIC MAN

It was then that Moreno obtained from the patriot *junta* the vote for the printing of a newspaper which should be a publicity sheet for the new government. Of this *Gaceta* he became the editor. It is through its pages that we become acquainted with the man.

He opened its columns for the expression of opinions by private individuals, which was unusual in a government publication, and he preached freedom of thought and speech in every issue. The paper was used also for the furthering of progressive movements. Editor Moreno believed in the education of the common people, which had been utterly neglected under Spanish rule. There is a record that Charles IV, the Spanish king deposed by Napoleon Bonaparte, had sent back to the colonies a petition for a school with the words, "I do not consider learning proper in America." Moreno asked for popular subscriptions for the library which was being started by the new government, and became its "protector," or, as we should say, "director." So Argentina honors him as the "father" of its great public library system.

To us of today who are discussing the democracies of the Americas as they have not been discussed for a hundred and more years, it is interesting to see what theories the different South American liberators had of the future of their continent. Moreno looked forward to exactly what has happened, the forming of several democratic states. In the absence of a king, he could not see why colonies which were so widely separated should be held under a single government. They should form separate governments, he thought, and make their constitutions independently. "How could we reach an understanding," he wrote, "with the Philippine Islands of which we have hardly any other information than that which is derived from a geographical chart? How could we reconcile our interests with those of a viceroyalty of Mexico?" There might come to be a federal system, he suggested, but the idea should be postponed.

We read these views and think how much trouble could have been avoided if they could have been adopted. Artigas would not have had to fight for his independent Uruguay, and Bolívar would not have broken his heart over the failure of his northern super-state.

Moreno was too democratic for his *junta*. He was so strongly opposed to dictatorship that he urged his associates to diminish the honors paid to their president. "If we desire that people should be free," he said, "we should scrupulously observe the sacred dogma of equality. If I consider myself equal to my fellow citizens, why should I present myself in a garb which indicates that they are less important than I am?" This could hardly be popular doctrine for people who loved pomp and show and parades and ceremonies.

Some say that Moreno's appointment as delegate of the *junta* to England was partly to get him out of the way because of differences of opinion. Be that as it may, he sailed at the end of January, 1811, on this important mission. But he was never to reach his destination. He had worn himself out by his hard work for the new government, and was not equal to the hardships of a stormy voyage. After four or five weeks at sea, he became ill and died. His last words, as reported by the secretaries who accompanied him, were, "Long live my country although I perish."

Argentina remembers Moreno as the "soul of the revolution of 1810," which established its independence. A

eulogy of him says that "under the guidance of his sur-
passing talent and copious knowledge, the press freely
scattered ideas upon all subjects concerning which the
American people were summoned to act when extricating
themselves from the rule of Spain. . . . With undaunted
front he fought prejudices, attacked abuses, and laid the
foundations of the Argentine Republic."

ARTIGAS OF URUGUAY

"Protector of Free Peoples"

SOMEWHERE about 1815 a Scotchman by the name of Robertson sailed up the Uruguay river to the camp of a patriot leader who was leading his people in a threefold struggle: a struggle against the patriot government at Buenos Aires, which would not allow his country complete self-government, against the emperor of Brazil, who wanted to acquire his territory, and against the king of Spain, who still claimed control of the colonies.

Here is his description of what he met at the end of that journey, as he wrote it to an English friend:

And there (I pray you do not turn sceptic on my hands), what do you think I saw? Why, the most excellent Protector of half of the New World, seated on a bullock's skull, at a fire kindled on the mud floor of his hut, eating beef off a spit, and drinking gin out of a cow-horn! He was surrounded by a dozen officers in weather-beaten attire, in similar positions, and similarly occupied with their chief. . . . The Protector was dictating to two secretaries, who occupied, at one deal table, the only two dilapidated rush-bottom chairs in the hovel.

To complete the incongruity of the scene, the floor of the one apartment of the mud hut (to be sure it was a pretty large one) in which the general, his staff, and secretaries were assembled, was strewn with pompous envelopes from all the provinces (some of them distant 1500 miles from that center of operations) addressed to "His Excellency the Protector."

At the door stood the reeking horses of couriers arriving every half hour, and the fresh ones of those departing as often. Soldiers, aides-de-camp, scouts, came galloping in from all quarters. . . . He received me not only with cordiality, but with what surprised me more, comparatively gentlemanlike manners . . . and really good breeding. The Protector's business was prolonged from morning till evening, and so were his meals; for, as one courier arrived another was dispatched, and as one officer rose from the fire at which the meat was spitted, another took his place.

AN ADVENTUROUS YOUTH

José Artigas, of whom we have this picture, was born in 1764, just forty years after his grandfather had been one of the first colonists of Montevideo, the city across the broad mouth of La Plata river from Buenos Aires on the northern side of the bay, in what is now Uruguay. Seven families went over from Buenos Aires in 1724 to start that new town. Each of these colonists was offered house lots in the town and large holdings in the "camp," as the wide acres of grassy plain are called, and a stock of two hundred head of cattle and one hundred sheep, as well as tools, supplies, and building materials. These pioneer settlers had to be sturdy fighting folk, for during the early period of the settlement there were frequent attacks by Indians, and there was always intermittent warfare with the Portuguese who came over from the territory of Brazil, just north.

South America is a land of violent and fascinating contrasts—in both scenery and men. Today we can leave the coast and river cities with their wide avenues, fine buildings, and harbors crowded with ships, and travel almost at once into the pampas, those miles upon miles of level grassy plains which are an ocean of land dotted with millions of animals. So in 1810 one had only to cross the Rio de la Plata to leave behind the university-trained patriot-leader Moreno, and find the gaucho chieftain, José Artigas, who grew up on the pampas in an atmosphere of war and violence.

As a youth in the wild hill country of the north, he became noted for his feats of strength and skilled horsemanship, as well as for his popularity as a leader of his companions. The political enemies of his later days declared that for a time the young man turned brigand, preying with his followers on the convoys of heavily laden horses and mules that passed to and fro from Argentina and the river valleys to Brazil. Doubtless he did engage in some smuggling, as was customary under the over-strict Spanish trade regulations. But the Spanish authorities could not have taken these activities very seriously, for he was chosen to be one of their mounted police in the region,—to guard against Indian attacks and prevent smuggling,—and in 1802 he became head of this force. Then in 1807 he served with his regiment against the British when they tried to take over some of the coastal section from Spain.

In 1810, the year of the Argentine declaration of independence, Artigas had a quarrel with a Spanish superior officer who threatened to discipline him by putting him in chains. He escaped by night in a small boat and made his way across the broad waters of the Plata to Buenos Aires, where he was welcomed by the Argentine leaders who were only too eager to send an expedition over to Montevideo and win the Uruguayan territory to the patriot cause.

If you look at the map, you will be reminded that Uruguay lies in a somewhat triangular section with the Plata river on the south, the Uruguay river on the west, Brazil to the northward, and the Atlantic ocean on the east. In Artigas's time, and earlier, this territory was known as *la Banda Oriental,* or "the Eastern Bank" of the

Uruguay river. It was far up on that river that Robertson went in 1815 to meet Artigas.

The story of the next few years is one of fighting, after Artigas's escape to Buenos Aires. The Spanish forces held Montevideo, after their expulsion from Buenos Aires, and there was much fighting. Moreover invaders from Brazil overran *la Banda Oriental,* claiming it for the royal family of Portugal which had come over to Brazil following Napoleon's moves against Portugal. The queen of Portugal, Carlotta, sister of the Spanish king Ferdinand, claimed the right to all Spanish colonial possessions in her brother's place, and there were those in both Montevideo and Buenos Aires who favored a monarchy instead of republics. But Artigas was not of their number. He and his fighting gauchos did valiant service in the wars, but from the first he differed with the leaders of the Buenos Aires *junta* as to the kind of government to be set up. The Buenos Aires men wanted a more centralized government, of which they were obviously to be in control. Artigas wanted each province to be self-governing, with a federation of all for certain purposes.

HIS "INSTRUCTIONS"

The crisis came in 1813. An assembly was called in Buenos Aires to which delegates were to come from all parts of the great viceroyalty, even as far inland and north as Upper Peru. Artigas sent his delegates with a set of famous "Instructions." They were to insist on complete

—: 125 :—

independence in local affairs. Each province was to organize its own government and retain its sovereignty. The United Provinces were to form a league of friendship for their "common defense, liberty, and mutual government," a kind of "League of Nations" with a central government, but no taxes or customs duties between the members. The plan followed obviously the pattern of our own Articles of Confederation and, to a lesser degree, the United States Constitution, both of which documents were studied by the South American leaders.

At the time when Artigas sent his five delegates, he was the recognized leader in Uruguay, and his armies were uniting with those from Buenos Aires in besieging the royalists in Montevideo. Yet the leaders of the assembly did not even admit the Uruguayan delegates, but sent them home with the excuse that their credentials were not in order. Naturally, General Artigas was furious. A short time later he withdrew his army from the siege of Montevideo, leaving the Buenos Aireans to carry on the attack alone. They were equally aroused, and retaliated by putting a price on his head. The break was final. Artigas was now the national leader for the territory which is now Uruguay, which he was determined to keep independent.

"PROTECTOR OF FREE PEOPLES"

The Uruguayans flocked to his standard, as did men from other provinces of the Spanish viceroyalty who did not wish to be governed by the Buenos Aires group. Artigas became known as the "Protector of Free Peoples,"

JOSÉ ARTIGAS
1764–1850
From the bust in the Gallery of Patriots, Washington, D. C.

his title when the English visitor found him in that rude
camp on the banks of the Uruguay river. In 1815 four
provinces besides his own had come under his banner.
When Montevideo fell, the men of Buenos Aires withdrew from the territory, having gotten rid of the Spaniards. Artigas was left the ruler for 350,000 square miles
of territory, and was defying both Brazilians and men
from Buenos Aires and the rest of southern Argentina.

His power could not last. He had no money, even to
equip and feed his soldiers. Yet for five years this rough,
self-made ruler held on against onslaughts of invading
Portuguese armies and attacks by the other patriot forces.
The men of the United Provinces were determined to gain
back the four provinces besides Uruguay which had gone
over to his side. His Uruguayans supported him to the
end in a desperate fight against hunger and hardship as
well as their enemies from without. At last he lost his final
battle, and in September, 1820, withdrew to Paraguay,
where he was allowed by Dictator Francia to remain, living quietly, to the end of a long life in 1850, at the age
of eighty-six.

Artigas had not succeeded in winning his independent
Uruguay, but he had seen the Spanish forces driven out of
the country. A dark and bloody period followed, with the
Portuguese taking possession of Montevideo and declaring
the land a part of Brazil. In 1825 a Uruguayan by the
name of Juan Antonio Lavalleja, with a band of thirty-
three followers took up the struggle for Uruguayan independence, a band known in South American annals as

the "Thirty-three Immortals." But the complete independence desired by Artigas did not come until 1830 when a separate government was approved jointly by Brazil and Argentina.

Artigas is remembered for the reply he made to a royalist agent of Spain who tried in the earlier days to persuade him to stay with the king's cause. "I cannot be purchased," he declared. "I wish no other reward for my hardihood than to see my nation free from Spanish rule; and if the noise of cannon cease during my lifetime, my hands will drop the sword which they have seized to defend my native land." That was the spirit in which he took up his second crusade to keep his people independent of other South American overlordship and so to be the "Protector of Free Peoples." On his tomb in Montevideo are inscribed the words, "Artigas, Founder of the Uruguayan Nation."

GENERAL BELGRANO OF ARGENTINA

"Hear, O Mortals, the sacred shouts
Of liberty, liberty, liberty!
Hear the sound of broken chains,
Behold equality enthroned;
Behold in face of day arising
A new and glorious nation."

From the Argentine National Hymn of May, 1813

THERE are two memorials to General Manuel Belgrano which together tell the story of his service in the Wars of Independence. One is a splendid mausoleum in Buenos Aires, which reminds his fellow-countrymen of the service he rendered in all Argentina. The other is far inland at Tucumán, a city of Upper Peru which is within the frontiers of the old Inca empire. Here in 1812 Belgrano won the great military victory of his career, the battle of Tucumán, which, according to the historians, saved the cause of revolution in Argentina and paved the way for the later victories of San Martín. If the royalist forces from central Peru had not been held back then, they could have swept across the continent to Buenos Aires and delayed the triumph of the cause of independence for years.

PATRIOT SOLDIER

Manuel Belgrano, who was born in Buenos Aires in 1770, was the son of wealthy Italian parents who had come out to Argentina. He studied at the local College of San Carlos and then went to Spain to study at the universities there. Returning to his native city, he had begun the practice of law when the British, early in the Napoleonic wars, desired commercial opportunities in South America, and took their chance to attack the Plata region. The Spanish viceroy was still governing in those years of 1806 and 1807, but the colonists had to take hold and defend their cities of Montevideo and Buenos Aires. Belgrano had had no training as a soldier, but he became a captain in the defending army. He was popular with his men, and went on from this military service to swing his soldiers to the cause of independence, after he had joined one of the secret societies and pledged himself to help to free his country.

When the patriot *junta* declared the independence of Argentina on May 25, 1810, Belgrano was one of the members, along with Mariano Moreno.* He took an active part in the new government, and was appointed by Moreno as head of an academy of mathematics which was founded at that time. It is interesting to know that he read all the histories of the American Revolution on which he could lay hold, and that George Washington was his especial hero. He had read Washington's Farewell Address so many times that he could repeat it from memory, and he translated it into Spanish so that his soldiers could read it.

After the Declaration of Independence, the patriots of Buenos Aires set themselves to revolutionize the rest of the viceroyalty and bring it into political union with them. We have read how the Uruguayans under Artigas did not fall in with that plan. The royalists at Asunción in Paraguay resisted such efforts, and Belgrano went against them with an army which was defeated in March, 1811. (However, the Paraguayans set up within two years a government completely independent of Spain, over which their General Francia ruled as dictator for a long period.)

AT TUCUMÁN
September 24, 1811

The most serious threat to the cause of independence lay in the northwest region of Upper Peru, through which

* See page 116.

Spanish forces from the western coast of Peru were being
sent to bring back into the fold the rebellious provinces of
La Plata. The royalist army had won victories and was
moving triumphantly on towards the Argentine region,
with the patriot army in retreat, when General Belgrano
disobeyed his orders. He was in command of the retreating army and had been ordered to continue that retreat
until he and his men reached safety in the city of Cordoba.

With the enemy's forces double in number to his own,
he turned back on them and won a complete victory near
the city of Tucumán, not only driving them back but
capturing their flags and cannon. South Americans like
to tell that the General's wife, Manuela, fought at her
husband's side in that fight and so distinguished herself
that she was made an officer in the army. Women as well
as men took their part in this struggle for independence
in the different colonies.

There is another pleasant story of that victory. As
Belgrano's troops were returning to the city after the battle,
they met a church procession on the streets carrying a
statue of the Virgin, "Our Lady of Mercy," whose feast
day it was. General Belgrano placed his baton in the
statue's hand as a sign of his reverent gratitude for his
victory. To this day in Tucumán, on the twenty-fourth
of September, the statue is taken from the church and
carried in the triumphal procession through the city, with
General Belgrano's baton still in the Virgin's right hand.

The Battle of Tucumán held the Spanish forces back
for the time, but in October, 1813, an army under Belgrano

MANUEL BELGRANO
1770–1820

was disastrously defeated. Early in 1814 San Martín came to the region to take Belgrano's place in command of the Army of the North. The two men met on the road, and became friends at once, with Belgrano insisting on yielding command to San Martín, whose military genius he admired.*

ARGENTINE INDEPENDENCE

Two more events in Belgrano's life should be remembered. He was one of two delegates sent to Spain in 1813 to try to arrange for self-government for Buenos Aires. These southern patriots would have been willing to have the province led as a monarchy by some member of the royal family, so long as it was independent and separate. But they were told that only surrender would be accepted, and were then ordered to leave Madrid. On his return, Belgrano suggested making a descendant of the Incas emperor for South America, but that scheme was rejected, as were many other ideas of the patriots.

It did become evident, however, that there must be a break with Spain, to whose king the provinces had been paying, since the 1810 Buenos Aires Declaration of Independence, a nominal allegiance. As San Martín stated the matter in a letter, it was "ridiculous to coin money, have a flag and a national cockade, and, lastly, to make war on a sovereign on whom it is believed that we are in a state of dependence." A congress was called at Tucumán to which Belgrano was appointed a delegate and in which

* See page 71.

he took an active part. On July 9, 1816, it declared the independence of the "United Provinces of La Plata," which were the provinces making up the present Argentina.

A portrait shows Belgrano as a handsome man, with regular features, dark hair loosely brushed back, and a determined chin. His eyes are steady, the expression of the face is strong and thoughtful. One can believe that he *was* the "brains and right arm" of the revolution, especially after the death of his friend Moreno.

BERNARDO O'HIGGINS OF CHILE

*Of a viceroy's son who became the
first President of the Republic of Chile*

IT starts in Ireland, this tale of the O'Higgins family,
father and son, as many another tale of famous
Americans has done. Sometime between 1740 and 1750
a barefoot boy who ran errands for the grand lady of the
Dangan Castle in County Meath in the southeast of Ireland, went to Cádiz in Spain on the invitation of an uncle

who was a priest and wanted to have him educated. He
was young Ambrose O'Higgins.

HIS FATHER—FROM EMIGRANT TO VICEROY

The young Irishman was a quick scholar, but when his
course of study was done, he did not want to take the
orders and become a priest. He had a roving foot and
longed to cross the ocean and see this New World of
which he had heard so much. His Spanish, which he had
just learned in his months of study, would help him in
the new country. He took passage to Buenos Aires, but
instead of settling there, continued on his journey, crossing the continent to Peru. There he became a humble
itinerant trader, selling goods as he traveled up and down
the Viceroyalty of Peru and south into Chile. In time he
bought his own little shop in Lima, Peru.

Before long, he became from his peddling an army con-
tractor, and was soon helping to build stations along the
road which was being constructed over the Andes. He
joined the army, and being a good fighting Irishman, did
well when he got a chance to strike some blows against
the Araucanians, those Indians of Chile who had not yet
been fully pacified after two hundred years. The Spanish
government began to take notice of him. He became an
army engineer, and then, in 1792, the Captain General of
Chile. But fast as these promotions were, they never went
beyond his abilities. He was an able and energetic official.
In Chile he set out at once, following his appointment,
to make a tour of the country, and did much to improve

BERNARDO O'HIGGINS
1778–1842
From the collection of Luis Alvarez Urquieta.

the wretched condition of the Indians who were leading a hard life of servitude in the mines and in the fields. He built two new cities to the south, constructed new roads, and had a new dyke put up to protect Santiago, now capital of Chile, from the flooding of its near-by river. To the relief of both sides, he managed, too, to settle the quarrel with the Araucanians and make a permanent peace.

So conspicuous was the work of this Irish-Spanish official in Chile that the government again took notice of him and made him Viceroy of Peru, a most important and surprising position for an outsider of Irish birth. Meanwhile he had taken to wife a Chilean lady, but he could not offer her church marriage because of the high Spanish office which he held. From this union came a son, Bernardo.

BERNARDO IN THE CHILEAN REVOLUTION

Young Bernardo, born in 1778, was sent by his father to England for his education, and there came under the influence of the South American patriots, joining, as Bolívar and San Martín had done, the "Gran Reunion Americana" established by Miranda. Returning to South America, he became an active member of the Chilean branch of this society, the strong and influential Lautaro Lodge. In Chile, as in the other provinces, there was a popular uprising when the news was received of Bonaparte's invasion of Spain. Their Independence Day was on September 18, 1810, matching the May 25th Declaration of Buenos Aires across the continent. Their first Congress met on July 4,

1811, in honor of our North American patriotic day, and Bernardo O'Higgins was the elected representative from the southern region, where he was soon to become the accepted patriot leader.

This Congress made many social reforms, such as freeing the slaves, setting up free trade, and reducing overhigh salaries of officials. This alarmed the wealthy families of Chile, the "old Spaniards," who feared that their power would slip under the new order. For the next few years there was always more or less civil war between different parties. Then in 1814 the royalist government which had won its victories in Peru dispatched an army to force Chile back into their viceroyalty, as it had been in former days. O'Higgins, who had been made commander of the army, fought a brave but losing battle against foes who far outnumbered him. He fled across the mountains to Mendoza, where General San Martín was building up his army.*

For several years the story of O'Higgins is closely interwoven with that of his chief, San Martín. Together they crossed the Andes, and entered Santiago, where Bernardo was made Director while San Martín went about the business of his intended expedition to Peru. Together they fought the battles of Chacabuco and then, a year later, of Maipú, by which the Spanish forces were driven out of Chile.

Our next picture of the Chilean leader is as he gathered a small navy for San Martín, while the latter was seeking

* See page 78.

aid in Buenos Aires. There is a tale of his standing on a high hill outside Santiago, his capital, and watching his first little fleet sail out on the Pacific. He shared San Martín's eagerness to drive the Spanish fleet from the Pacific and carry an army on these new ships northward to free Peru. Chile gained under him the honor of having the first navy of any of the South American republics.

AS "SUPREME DIRECTOR"

In 1818 O'Higgins declared the complete independence of Chile from Spain, and became the first executive of the freed republic. He was a man of San Martín's age, well educated and a clear thinker, with theories of the way that his people must be trained towards the republican form of government. Popular rule was his ideal, although he felt himself forced to take autocratic control.

Chile had suffered from the break-down of law and order during the long struggle for independence. O'Higgins set up an excellent system of rural and city police, put night watchmen on the streets of Santiago, and installed a street lighting system there. The country grew quiet and safe as the bands of roving brigands were brought under control.

He encouraged agriculture, completed an important irrigation canal to redeem the land around Maipú, and did his best to build up trade. But education was his special interest. A school director who advocated the English system of schools, known as the Lancastrian method, came out from London to Chile, and O'Higgins welcomed the new ideas, which were at that time being introduced also into New England and other parts of the eastern United States.

If he had kept safely to educational reforms, O'Higgins might have kept his office longer. But he introduced unpopular measures by which he sought to take away some of the land privileges of the aristocracy, and abolished cock fighting, bull fighting, and other amusements connected with gambling. There were jealousies, too, among the other Chilean leaders, and a fear that he intended to make himself dictator. He tried to gather a congress to create a constitution, but felt obliged to get his own delegates elected for the carrying out of his plans. Uprisings took place all over the country, and in January, 1823, he was asked to resign.

He went into exile in Peru, and lived there until 1842, the year of his death, an honored and highly respected guest of the Peruvian republic. Chile had hard years of civil strife between its would-be leaders following his withdrawal, and was inviting him back in 1842 when news of his death came. One of the most picturesque and sincerely patriotic leaders of those days, O'Higgins has later won from a grateful republic more honor than was accorded to him in his lifetime.

BOLÍVAR, THE GREAT LIBERATOR

THE BOYHOOD OF BOLÍVAR

"Is there any man living capable of freeing South America from Spain?"—Bolívar's question to Humboldt

ONE name stands out, written so large across the pages of South American history that all other names are dwarfed beside it—that of Simón Bolívar. In his native state, Venezuela, there is hardly a town so small that it does not have a statue of the national hero standing in a central plaza or square bearing his name. Coins are named for him, and his portrait looks out from postage stamps as frequently as does that of our own George Washington in the United States. Indeed, the place of the two men in the affections and honor of their compatriots is similar, in spite of the many differences in their lives. As Washington led the colonies in their fight for freedom, so Bolívar led at least four of the South American republics in winning their independence, while all South America, from the Isthmus of Panama to Cape Horn, owed much to the inspiration he gave them in freeing the continent early in the nineteenth century from the overlordship of Spain.

Yet how little anyone suspected his future greatness in his childhood and youth! Certainly the anxious relatives who tried to take the place of his parents for the orphaned boy, had no such idea. To them he was, as one of his uncles once remarked, like a *polvorin,* a horn of powder, and young Simón responded, with his usual quickness, "Then be careful not to come near me. I might explode."

HIS FAMILY

Simón Bolívar was born in Caracas July 24, 1783, in the year when the North American colonies were closing their Revolutionary War and winning independence from their mother country. His father died when he was three years old, and his gentle, lovely mother, who had always somewhat spoiled the handsome youngster, died before he was seven. To his father he is said to have owed his name, that name which we must twist around our English-trained tongues if we are to give the proper Spanish pronunciation, with Simón turned to a musical See-moán, with the stress on the final syllable, and Bolívar, with the accent in the middle, as if it were spelled Bol-eé-var. The father's part came in the name itself. Six days after his birth he was taken, as a high-born child should be, to the Cathedral to be christened, and there the uncle, his mother's brother, joined with th. priest in wanting him given the name of the saint on the eve of whose feast he was born. But the father insisted instead on the name of his own first ancestor in South America, the Simón Bolívar who came out to the new country two hundred years before and became one of the founders of the city of Caracas, as well as an honored official of the king's government, sent once to Spain to report on an important mission.

It was a good name for the boy who was to take pride in being thoroughly South American, as well as in his Spanish ancestry and connections. But one of the first lessons the proud, headstrong youth had to learn, as he grew older, was that he and his people were colonials, "creoles" as all Spaniards born in South America were called, and that a creole was looked down upon by the Spanish officials sent out by the king to govern his rich colonies. A creole boy might have noble blood in his veins, as did young Simón. He might be very wealthy, as Simón was. He might go to Spain for his education, as Simón did when he was older. But in his native land he could never hold any high office or win any of the freedom in business or social life which belonged to the Spanish-born aristocracy without question.

Simón Bolívar rebelled always against authority. He was an affectionate lad, easily led by those he loved and admired but quick-tempered and impatient when crossed. He was a boy whom everyone noticed, for he was handsome, slender of build, tremendously active and energetic, with a smile which won him friends, a head of curly, black hair, and brilliant, deep-set dark eyes. His gentle young mother yielded always to his demands, as did his two sisters who were a few years older. The uncle, Miguel José Sanz, who took over the care of him after his mother's death, was a distinguished judge, but too busy and easygoing to have much influence over the lively boy. He furnished him with tutors, who trained his quick mind and disciplined him as much or as little as they found convenient and not too difficult. One, Simón Rodriguez, became his friend and companion and had much to do with shaping his thoughts and his later life.

WITH RODRIGUEZ, HIS TUTOR

It was a curious friendship, for Rodriguez was a strange man, an intellectual eccentric, who would not have appealed to most boys. His appearance was rough and uncared for, his manners uncouth. But there burned within him an intellectual fire which attracted the eager, restless boy. With him Simón went to one of the family estates in the Aragua Valley, at the end of the beautiful lake of Valencia, where he led a strenuous, out-of-door life of mountain climbing, following trails through the forests, and learning to ride and to handle his body in active, manly sports and exercises. To those years, with their journeyings in the Venezuelan uplands, Simón Bolívar owed the strong, wiry body that served him so well in his later military life. He could always outwalk, outclimb, and outdo in physical endurance most of his soldiers, though they were reckoned hardy men.

This tutor did more than help him to train and toughen the muscles of his body. Rodriguez had wandered all over Europe during the years of the French Revolution. He always carried in his pocket a copy of one or another of Rousseau's famous, new books on education and the rights of man, and shared its ideas with his young pupil as they went on their long walking trips. He was getting new books of this kind, too, smuggled into the colonies in spite of the strict government censorship.

Later, it was easy for Bolívar to trace back some of his ideas to this teacher who lived with him for these eight years. At the time they made only a passing impression on the boy, but he remembered them when Rodriguez was forced, in Simón's fifteenth year, to flee the country because he was suspected of being mixed up in an attempt at revolution which was quickly suppressed. Then the boy went back to San Mateo and became, as his father's son should, a cadet in the regiment of the Militia of Whites, picking up some small information in the art of waging war and taking great satisfaction in his smart uniform.

IN SPAIN AND FRANCE

Meanwhile one of his uncles had gone to Spain, and soon sent for his nephew to come to be with him. So young Simón, not yet seventeen years old, sailed for Spain to finish his education there, as he would probably have done much sooner if his father had lived. It was a great experience for the lad who had never been anywhere abroad, to make the long trip. The ship put in at Vera Cruz, and he rode two hundred miles on horseback to Mexico City and met there the viceroy and the archbishop, who were interested, according to accounts, in the wealthy young aristocrat, but somewhat annoyed by his questions and his ideas of American independence. Cuba, which was the ship's next stop, was seething with revolutionary ideas. In Spain he landed in Bilbao, the home region of the first Simón Bolívar, and there saw his first wheeled vehicle. (The steep paths of Venezuela allowed only for horses and mules, not carts or carriages.) In it he rode to Madrid, to the uncle who was a favorite of Queen Maria Luisa and an officer of the Royal Guard. He was introduced into the gay life of the capital and court and plunged into it head over heels for seven months. Then he turned to the education for which he had come, learning French, English, and Italian—languages which were to serve him well in his later life.

He fell in love, too, with a beautiful young girl, daughter of a nobleman and niece of a prominent Venezuelan, and was eager to be married at once. As she was but fifteen and he barely eighteen, the father insisted on delay.

He went to Paris, where Napoleon was setting up his Republic, with himself as First Consul. For the time, Napoleon was his hero, worshiped with all the ardor of his nature, and he studied the republican form of government, which he saw in working form here for the first time.

But sorrow and disappointment were in store for him. He returned to Madrid, married his Maria Teresa, and took her to his ancestral home in Venezuela, where they spent a thoroughly happy ten months. Then she died suddenly of a fever, and young Bolívar returned to Madrid utterly crushed and grief-stricken. His boyhood was over, and yet he was hardly more than a boy in years.

The tale of his life during the next few years belongs to our story only as we watch the awakening of the desire to lead his home colonies to independence. He was forced to leave Madrid because his uncle came suddenly into disfavor, but already he had begun to see that a creole from the colonies could not go far in Spanish life at court, and could not hope to be sent back to his native land in any official position. That kind of honor belonged only to the Spanish-born. In Paris in 1804 he watched Napoleon throw off all pretense of a republican form of government and crown himself emperor. His hero worship was abruptly ended.

"I used to adore him as hero of the Republic, as the brilliant star of glory and the genius of liberty!" he told his cousin, Fanny de Villars. "I knew of nobody in the past to be compared with him, nor did the future seem to promise his equal. But he made himself emperor and from that day I have looked upon him as a hypocritical tyrant."

We shall remember this when Bolívar refuses again and again any title of ruler when it is offered to him after his military triumphs. He was willing to be called the "Liberator" but nothing more.

Already in these days there are hints of the turn his thoughts were taking. There is the story of his meeting with Alexander von Humboldt, the famous naturalist who had recently returned from his explorations in Venezuela and adjoining regions.

"Is South America ripe for independence from Spain?" young Bolívar is said to have asked.

"Yes," answered Humboldt.

"Is there any man living capable of freeing South America from Spain?"

"No," he replied, little guessing that the young man who stood before him was to do that splendid task.

THE OATH OF MONTE SACRO

At about this time Bolívar became twenty-one years of age and inherited a huge sum of money. With the abandon which was characteristic of him he threw himself into a gay and dissipated life, gambling away his money and almost ruining his health. But the period of gayety was soon over, and he turned from it to earnest study. He found that his old tutor Rodriguez was living in poverty in Vienna, and went and got him and brought him to

SIMÓN BOLÍVAR
1783–1830
After M. N. Bate, Lenox Library, New York.

Paris. Together in the next year or two they went on long walking tours through France, Switzerland, Spain and Italy, talking always of the problems of government and the hope of independence for South America. In these months Bolívar was becoming a man of one purpose, a patriot with the overwhelming longing to free his native land. That purpose came to its high moment one afternoon as the two friends sat on Monte Sacro, the hill outside Rome where the plebeians of the ancient city had been wont to meet two thousand years before when they were seeking to maintain their rights.

There the two men sat and looked out over the city. They made a strange contrast, the older man in rough, worn garments, a long-haired dreamer with eyes that looked far beyond the immediate scene, and the younger, alert, eager, impassioned, with his slender, patrician figure and his deep-set black eyes and shock of black hair. Rodriguez sat on a block of marble and watched his young friend as he walked up and down, driven by the thoughts within. Then all at once, after a period of silence, Bolívar fell to his knees, and spoke with his right hand uplifted.

"Rodriguez," he said, "I swear before you, I swear by the God of my forefathers, I swear by my forefathers and by my native country, that I shall never allow my hands to be idle, nor my soul to rest until I have broken the shackles which chain us to Spain."

That was the oath as Bolívar used to repeat it in his later years, when he looked back to this moment on Monte Sacro as the beginning of his new life. From that hour he did not rest. Within the year he sailed from Europe, stopping in the United States on his homeward journey, and visiting the cities of Boston, New York, Philadelphia, and lastly Charleston, South Carolina. From that port he sailed for Venezuela, landing there near the end of the year 1806. There he found that the seeds of revolution had already been sown by another South American patriot, Miranda.

EARLY SERVICE FOR INDEPENDENCE

1806-1812

In Caracas, young Bolívar heard of the failure of Miranda's *Leander* expedition of that same year, 1806, and only wished that he had returned in time to meet the veteran soldier. He found his brother, Juan Vicente Bolívar, and others of the young patriots, to be meeting frequently to discuss what could be done towards independence. They were the sons of creoles, and represented some of the wealthiest native South American families. The Bolívar brothers entertained this group frequently in their home at San Mateo, but no move was made for action.

Then on May 5, 1808, that event happened in Europe which was to give the start to the South American Wars of Independence. Murat, Napoleon's brother-in-law, marched with his armies on Madrid, massacred hundreds of Spanish subjects on the "Bloody Third of May," (as history names it) and two days later put Joseph Bonaparte on the throne of Spain. We have read in the story of Miranda of the coming of that news to Caracas. Simón

Bolívar was one of the young men who marched the streets and entered the palace, shouting "Down with the French Usurper! Long live Ferdinand!"

Now the secret meetings became more impassioned. The speeches were revolutionary. Simón discovered that he had a talent for speaking which his patriot uncle, "Uncle Ribas," as he is always called, and some of the older leaders recognized. When on April 19, 1810, the patriot *junta* deposed the viceroy, Bolívar was named lieutenant colonel of the militia. At a meeting of the *junta* he made a speech urging an appeal for help to England, and offered a part of his fortune to finance such a trip for him and two companion delegates.*

This official mission was not particularly successful. Lord Wellesley was ready to help the new government if it was actually threatened by France, but could not treat with it as an independent state. But Bolívar went from it to Miranda's house, and persuaded the old warrior that the time had come for his return to lead the South American revolution.

HIS FIRST SPEECH

The tale of their return to Caracas is told in the story of Miranda. In those early days of the revolution and of the First Republic, Bolívar was always second to the older man. Yet we get pictures of the fiery young patriot along the way. It was he who made the speech on July Fourth, 1811, which led to the resolution for independence pre-

* See page 46.

sented and passed by the Congress the following day.

The discussion had centered about the delays in the National Congress during its four months of meetings. The fiery young Bolívar leaped to his feet and spoke:

> There are not two congresses. What we desire is that this union should become effective and should urge us on to the glorious enterprise of our liberty. To unite ourselves in order to repose, to sleep in the arms of apathy, was yesterday a disgrace. *Today it is treason.*
>
> The National Congress is debating what decision should be reached. And what do its members say? . . . That we should await the results of the policy of Spain. What does it matter whether Spain sells her slaves to Napoleon or keeps them, if we are resolved to be free? You say that great projects must be prepared during the calm. *Were not three hundred years of calm enough? Do they desire that we wait for three hundred more?*
>
> The Patriotic Society respects, as it should, the National Congress, but Congress should heed the Patriotic Society, which is the center of the revolutionary interests. Let us fearlessly lay the corner stone of South American liberty. To hesitate is to be lost. I move that a committee from this body lay these sentiments before the sovereign Congress.

The motion was carried with enthusiasm. The resolution was drawn up on this fourth day of July, the thirty-fifth anniversary of the Declaration of Independence of the American colonies, and passed the next day. When word spread from the audience chamber to the street, the city went wild with delight. Venezuela was to be free. Jubilant young men dashed through the streets tearing down the portraits of Ferdinand VII and trampling them underfoot. Bolívar was one of their leaders.

TWO EPISODES

The story of Bolívar's relations with Miranda is fully told in our life of the older man.* Yet from these years of the young man's first service to his country there remain certain episodes that belong in our portrait of him. At the time of the earthquake of March 26, 1812, Bolívar rushed into the streets and began at once to aid the wounded and dying. As he was pulling with all his strength at heavy beams which imprisoned the victims, he heard the cry of some of the royalist priests: "This is the Judgment of God! Pray to be forgiven for driving out the representatives of His Holy Majesty, the King of Spain! Down with the Republic!" The shock of the earthquake had almost unnerved the young man. This cry, with the wailing response of the people, was the final horror. Turning upon those nearest to him, he shook his fist and shouted the words which have never been forgotten: "If Nature opposes us, we will battle with her, too, and compel her to obey us!"

One other phrase, used not by him but of him, is to be remembered. He had fought in the battles of the First Republic; he had had the fortress of Puerto Cabello betrayed by members of his own garrison and had returned to Miranda heart-broken at his failure. He had resented Miranda's surrender, and taken the older man's sword

* For the account of these years, see pages 46-61.

from him in the dark of the night and been among those who led him away to a prison cell. The Spaniards had gained possession of that prison, and Miranda was their captive. Friends interceded that Bolívar should be allowed to go into exile, and the Spanish commander, Monteverde, spoke the contemptuous words which must have eaten into his soul: "Pay no attention to the fool. Give him his passport and let him go." With those words ringing in his ears, the young patriot left his native land.

THE LIBERATOR WINS HIS TITLE

"I regard the title of Liberator as more glorious and satisfying than the scepters of all the empires on earth."—Bolívar

THINGS looked exceedingly dark for the patriot cause on that August day in 1812 when Simón Bolívar, with a few of his fellow soldiers, escaped from Caracas after Miranda's imprisonment and sailed to the little Dutch-controlled island of Curaçao, one of the Leeward Islands just north from the coast of Venezuela.

But Monteverde had not reckoned with two forces that were at work in the impetuous, ardent American, with his long, haggard face and dark, piercing eyes. One was his passion for freedom for South America, dating from his early youth and sharpened to intensity by the experiences and dreams of these last years. The other was his amazing power of leadership. One wonders whether the young officer himself recognized this power as yet. His enthusiasm was contagious. He was soon to show how he could take a handful of men and so inspire them that they would follow him through untold hardships and manage, with him, to snatch victory from defeat.

"Often," wrote one of his generals at a later time, "I go to him full of bitterness. Only to see him disarms me and I come away full of admiration."

It is this growing power that we watch as we follow him through these early years of the Wars of Independence.

A BOLD PLAN

1812

Bolívar left Caracas in August. In November he was back on South American soil—not in Venezuela, for that land was still under Monteverde's rule, but in the neighboring province of New Granada. This was the northwestern part of the continent, as Venezuela was the northeastern. It was to take, within Bolívar's lifetime, the name Colombia.

Here in the seaport of Cartagena there still remained a patriot government, and in other parts of the province the revolt against the Spanish royalists had been successful. Looking out from the island of Curaçao Bolívar saw New Granada as the one spot where the patriot cause still held a foothold. So he came to it, having conceived the daring project of reconquering Venezuela with the help of these revolutionists.

No project ever looked less likely to win favor and support. Bolívar was a stranger here, but the news of the failure of the Venezuelan republic had come ahead of him, with probably the report of his own military defeat. There may have been the ugly rumor, too, of Bolívar's part in Miranda's capture by the Spanish. There was a certain amount of civil war in the province, but no strong united movement for a widespread revolution against

Spain. If the citizens had not united to free themselves, how could they be inspired to free a sister province?

Bolívar went as soon as he landed to the patriot-dictator of Cartagena, a young man of twenty-four by the name of Camilo Torres. Bolívar was at this time twenty-nine years of age but he looked older. He had suffered much in the recent campaigns. He had been ill and his face was white with an alarming pallor, with deep wrinkles in the skin. But from that thin, haggard face the dark, piercing eyes shone out with startling effect.

He poured out his plan to the young governor, and Torres listened, at first indifferently, then with interest balanced by doubt, and at last eagerly, swept away by the fire of Bolívar's eloquence. They talked for hours, and when Bolívar went away he had the governor's consent to some such move as he desired. But, said Torres, the people of Cartagena must first be won over to the plan.

THE CARTAGENA PLEA

That was enough, and more than enough for the Venezuelan. He rushed back to his lodgings and wrote pages upon pages in defense of the undertaking. First he gave the reasons for the failure of the Miranda government, then reviewed the mistakes of the revolution, and wound up with a fiery plea for immediate action. The New Granadans must make such a move for their own self-defense, he argued. Spain had conquered the neighboring province and would soon be coming over the mountains. If the patriots delayed, reinforcements would soon be pouring in from Spain, and the chance for victory would be lost. If they moved now, they would find the Venezuelan rebels rallying to their cause.

"It is a sure thing," he wrote, "that the moment we appear in Venezuela, we shall be joined by thousands of valiant patriots who long to see us arrive, in order to throw off the yoke of their tyrants and to unite their forces with ours in defense of liberty."

Now for the first time he used this word Colombia, which he was later to give to the three northern republics of our own time, Venezuela, Colombia, and Ecuador, in his vain attempt to unite the three into a single American nation. It was a name Miranda had suggested, and it caught attention. The honor and the glory of New Granada demanded, he declared, that she assume the tasks of "liberating the cradle of *Colombian* independence" and freeing the people of Caracas. "Let us hasten to break the chains of those victims who groan in their dungeons, ever awaiting their salvation at your hands. Do not abuse their confidence. Do not remain insensible to the lamentations of your brothers. Fly quickly to avenge the dead; to give life to the dying, freedom to the oppressed, and liberty to all."

The plea was signed by his name alone—"From the Venezuelan Colonel, Simón Bolívar, to the People of Cartagena." He had it printed and distributed on the streets and in the public places. Then a few hours later he slipped out from his lodging and walked the streets, an unknown stranger, waiting, watching, listening, hoping.

Groups of men were standing on the street corners with copies of the pamphlet in their hands, and they were talking with animation. Bolívar walked slowly past them, listening. "He is right," some were saying, and others nodded their heads in agreement. "The Venezuelan talks sense," others said; and still others, "It is true what he says." Bolívar went back to his lodgings with a heart full of rejoicing. He had won the people. They were going to support him.

ON THE MAGDALENA RIVER

His joy was short-lived. He was given no military forces of his own, but was allowed to enlist in the army and was then put immediately under the authority of a military commander, a Frenchman, who heartily disliked the young colonel and was jealous of him. This man promptly sent him to an unimportant post over on the Magdalena River, away from all the fighting that was going on along the coast, and told him on no account to make any move until he had instructions. Once more Bolívar was side-tracked, as he had been in Venezuela.

But at that remote fort he found four hundred soldiers, men without training, undisciplined, and in ragged old uniforms. He went to work at once to give them training. Day after day he drilled them, keeping them at their practice until they were ready to drop in their tracks. With any other man they might have mutinied, but not with Bolívar. He won their utmost devotion to himself and to the cause of liberty.

Bolívar looked over, too, the region where he was stationed. The Magdalena river led through swampy jungle and tropical forest up from the sea to the lower reaches of the Cordilleras and the high inland plateau. Along its reaches the explorer Quesada had made his difficult way in the search for El Dorado. Now its upper towns and forts were in possession of royalists who were able to keep the patriot forces of the inland regions from any contact with those on the seacoast. Bolívar made his plans. His French commander was off fighting on the coast. Without a sign of an order from headquarters, Bolívar set off on a fighting expedition with his trained men up the river.

It was a mad adventure, but it succeeded. The royalists were taken completely off their guard by this sudden and utterly unexpected attack. In the first town he entered, he captured ammunition and boats which he used to good effect as he moved on to the fort next higher up the river. In the course of a fortnight of daring attacks he captured the line of fortified towns extending to the foot of the mountains and left them in control of their patriot citizens.

It was a difficult adventure. The region was swampy, with jungles extending to the river's edge. The men had to fight their way through almost impassable forest stretches. Bolívar caught a malarial fever which so weakened him that by the time they came to the last town he was shaking with chills and fever and could hardly stand.

But he did not give up to illness until the last fort was in his possession.

Then he made a clever move. Knowing his danger of court-martial and dismissal from the army, he wrote a glowing account of his successes not to his immediate military superiors but to the government and people of Cartagena. He had appealed to them before. He reasoned rightly that the victories would speak for themselves, and took occasion to urge that his original plan be now put into effect. Now could not he and his men, with other troops, march on to the rescue of the towns on the Venezuelan border, whose defender, Castillo, was already being attacked by the Spaniards?

"Are you content," Bolívar wrote, "to sit and wait for the invader to strike and then try to rouse the patriots to repel them? Or will you allow me to strike by taking my force up the river and across the mountains to Castillo, joining forces with him, and then march on to Venezuela?"

ACROSS THE ANDES, AND ON TO CARACAS

There were objections, but Bolívar met them all. His enthusiasm carried the people with him, and his men were ready to follow wherever he led. Within a month the little army started off on one of those terrific mountain marches which are always to be remembered in connection with Bolívar.

It was a heart-breaking journey which they had before them. A glance at a map shows the great range of high mountains which lay between them and the Venezuelan valleys, but no map can show that lofty wall of rock which they must scale. These soldiers came up from the hot plains where they had been resting after their river fighting. They were utterly unused to the terrific cold, the bitter, piercing winds, and the thin air of the mountain heights. Gasping for breath and sick with the painful mountain sickness, they had to climb sheer precipices where a single misstep meant death in the deep gorges below.

The region was uninhabited and they ran short of food. Without their leader the four hundred men who survived could never have accomplished that terrible march. But Bolívar was everywhere along the long line, helping, encouraging, cheering them on to new efforts. They fought an opposing Spanish force at a point high in the mountains and came through. At last, a weary, haggard, emaciated band, they reached the green slopes of the valleys. But they could not stop to recuperate. They must move on, fighting their way as they went.

The campaign which followed was a bitter one, marked with cruelty on both sides. In the ninety days from their start in New Granada to their victorious entry into Caracas the little army marched seven hundred and fifty miles, fought six battles, and recaptured the western part of Venezuela from the Spaniards who had occupied it.

They came to Caracas, and there Bolívar had the first of those public triumphs which were an utter satisfaction to his soul. He had watched Napoleon have his triumphs in France and Italy. Now his own turn had come, and the affair was carried through in dramatic fashion which was as satisfying to the Spanish-American people as to their hero. Across from the little river Guaira, Bolívar put off his worn fighting clothes and donned a uniform of white and blue, rich with gold braid and stars. At the south gate of the city he dismounted from his white horse. An arch of flowers had been erected beyond the bridge, and he and his war-worn young veterans passed under it. A committee of citizens escorted him to a two-wheeled chariot which was surrounded by young girls in white. They showered laurel wreaths and flowers upon him. Then twelve young beauties, daughters of the nobility of the city, took hold of the silken ropes and drew the car slowly through the city streets.

Cannon thundered, church bells rang, bands played, and men and women went wild with joy as the procession wound through the town over flower-carpeted streets, with Bolívar standing in the chariot, bowing to right and left. Forgotten were the hardships behind and the difficulties ahead as the crowd paid honor to their hero, shouting: "The Liberator! Hail the Liberator! Long live Bolívar!"

DARK DAYS

The triumphs of Bolívar were always followed quickly with disaster. He set up the Second Republic of Venezuela, which was to run a short and difficult course because of the dissensions among the leaders. Bolívar had made his speech disclaiming any desire to be a dictator.

> The General who has led the liberating hosts to victory will not ask any other reward than of sharing your dangers and bearing your arms wherever there are tyrants. His mission is finished. To restore American dignity, so barbarously outraged; to re-establish the free forms of republican government; to break your chains: these have been the constant aims of all his efforts. . . . Nothing shall separate me, Venezuelans, from my first and only intentions: your liberty and glory.

An assembly of "notable, wise, and virtuous men" was to be solemnly convoked to set up the government. Meanwhile he and his armies set out to fight. There were victories over the Spaniards in some sections, but some defeats. The Council of Caracas made him General-in-Chief and bestowed on him officially the title of "Liberator." He accepted it, saying, "I regard it as more glorious and satisfying than the scepters of all the empires on earth." He tried to appease his fellow-officers and rivals by establishing an "Order of Liberators" and even went so far as to send one of its emblems to General Marino, leader in eastern Venezuela as he had been in the western section. Marino had won victories there against the Spaniards and was not likely to be willing to share any honors.

But all this time the Spanish royalists were gathering their forces. Soon there was to come on the scene a new and terrible leader, with a new army. This was Boves, a

BOLÍVAR, SOLDIER AND STATESMAN
Palacio Federal en Caracas.

Spanish pirate and smuggler, who had chosen the side of the royalists and had gone into the *llanos,* the great grassy plains of the country, to recruit his men. These great plains, sloping down from the mountains along the river valleys, are today the cattle country of Venezuela. In those days, they were a wild region inhabited by groups of half-civilized men, part Indian, part negro, part of mixed blood, who lived their lives on horseback taming the cattle and horses that ranged the open grass-lands.

These were the men whom Boves gathered into an army and led in the fight for Spain in a warfare more terrible than any that South America had known. To this day the memory of those days lingers in Venezuela, and the name of Boves is spoken as that of Attila the Hun was spoken in Europe in the Dark Ages. For six months the patriots fought against him, but it was a losing fight in spite of Bolívar's terrific energy and skill in campaigning. There came at last, a time when this avenging army, which massacred civilians as well as fighters, was moving on Caracas, and Bolívar came to the bitter knowledge that the city must be abandoned.

The story of the twenty-day flight of the frightened, escaping people, with Bolívar riding sadly with them, is one of the epics of disaster in the world's history. He could do nothing for the men, women, and children who were perishing before his eyes on the terrible mountain journey and in the swampy jungles between the heights. It was the rainy season, and the sufferings of these city dwellers, who had never left their homes before, were an agony to the man who rode at the head of that line which started with ten thousand souls and ended with only a small surviving remnant.

They came to the coast, and Bolívar found himself blamed for the tragedy, though others had failed him because they would not coöperate in his plans and efforts. The leaders were all quarreling among themselves over the spoils which had been brought from the city, the silver vessels which Bolívar had taken to keep them from falling into the hands of the enemy. He was accused of being a traitor. Heartsick, despairing, he and General Marino, the leaders in the west and east, went aboard a vessel that was putting out to sea. For the second time Bolívar was an exile, now with a war-torn, ruined country behind him.

He went back to Cartagena, where he had started on the disastrous undertaking, and on to Tunja, where the Congress of New Granada was meeting. President Torres received him warmly and refused to listen to his bitter self-reproaches. The soldiers along the route cheered him as if he were returning in triumph instead of defeat. When he came before the Congress, he begged to be allowed to remain standing like a prisoner before the bar, but Torres drew him up on the platform to the seat beside himself. He told his long story of battles and defeats, and Torres made his answer:

General Bolívar, your country is not dead so long as your sword exists; with it you will return to redeem her from the dominion of her oppressors. . . . You have been an unfortunate soldier, but you are a great man.

New Granada was in a better state than unhappy Venezuela, and independence might have come to these northern countries of South America by a continuation of these patriot attacks during the next months and years, if there had not been a shift of power in Europe. Napoleon fell, defeated by the English, and was banished to Elba. His brother was put off the throne of Spain, and Ferdinand VII, the deposed king, came out of imprisonment to resume his rule. The Regency which had carried on the government for him had been wise in granting some degree of independence to the South American colonies, thus hoping to keep the royalists in power and hold the empire together. Ferdinand would have none of such pacifying measures. Spanish troops had been freed from fighting in France and against Napoleon. He prepared an expeditionary force of fifteen thousand men, with ammunition and reinforcements, which was to suppress all revolts and move from the north down through all the Spanish-American colonies as far as Buenos Aires, bringing them back into the empire. Nor did he forget to give special orders for the capture and death of Bolívar, as arch-enemy of Spain.

This was the first real army that had been sent out from Spain, and the patriot governments could not stand up against it. Bolívar escaped to Jamaica when the New Granadan fort which he was defending was taken. The armies came up the Magdalena river and captured the capital city of New Granada and ordered six hundred of its leading citizens shot down in groups in the public square as an example to all rebels. Bolívar's friend, President Torres, was executed, and the government completely taken over by the royalists.

All this news came to Bolívar in Jamaica, where he was living by borrowing from day to day, merely existing in an uncomfortable, squalid little hut. Even here he narrowly escaped assassination. He went out one night and came back to find one of his friends dead in the hammock where he usually slept. A knife intended for Bolívar had been driven into his heart in the darkness. The Spanish government reached out its long arm to hunt down all the patriot leaders, and Bolívar was the leader of leaders.

In those Jamaica days Bolívar came to the lowest ebb of his career. He was ill, worn to the shadow of his former self, and the gay courage which had never failed him when he was among his friends seemed to them to be gone. The sympathetic British governor, seeing him one day, remarked sadly: "The flame has absorbed the oil!"

A LETTER TO THE WORLD

That flame was to flare up with a brilliant spurt. An Englishman, hearing Bolívar talk, asked that he write down his hopes and plans for his country. He made the request an excuse for writing a lengthy epistle which went to friends in England, and in the United States.

This Jamaica letter shows Bolívar at his best. It shows the new, mature Bolívar, who had come through the bitterness of defeat and arrived at a sure purpose and faith.

He has gone beyond the idea of a free Venezuela and a free New Granada and is thinking of the continent as a whole. He discusses the probable future of Chile, Peru, and the Plata region as well as the northern provinces. All must throw off the Spanish yoke. South America must be free and independent. There will probably, he thinks, be several republics, each with strong central authority. The Venezuela experiences have convinced him that the people are not ready for genuinely democratic government, after the pattern laid down in the United States. They have been too long under oppressive rule, and have not had the political training of their brothers of the north.

There the letter might have stopped, and it would have commanded our interest and admiration. We should have remembered that it was written by a man discredited and in exile at a time when there was not a single independent government left on the South American continent, and admired his courage and faith.

But Bolívar does not stop there. He goes on to prophesy concerning the whole Pan-American future. He sees the possibility of the Americas as one. It would be less difficult, he thinks, to unite the two American continents than to reconcile Americans and Spaniards. He dreams of a union of all the republics of America, not for governmental purposes but for conference and mutual support. "I wish to see," he wrote, "the formation in America of the greatest nation in the world." He added a prophecy that has not yet, even in this twentieth century, been fulfilled, although it looks nearer to fulfillment than at any time since he made it. He saw the Americas as one, treating with the powers of the rest of the world.

"May we some day be fortunate enough to install there at Panama an august Congress composed of representatives, kings, and empires, that may deal with and discuss the high interests of peace and war with the nations of the other three parts of the world?"

Rarely does a man wield equal power with the pen and with the sword. Bolívar wrote during his lifetime three papers which are still quoted in the legislative halls of the South American republics, as the Declaration of Independence and Washington's Farewell Address are quoted in our own Congress. One was the Cartagena call to arms to free the colonies from Spanish rule, the second was this open letter with its survey of the Americas, the third was the Constitution of Angostura, drawn up for the third Venezuelan Republic. On them rests part of his title to enduring fame.

BACK TO SOUTH AMERICA

When Bolívar wrote the Jamaica letter he was an exile, penniless and with a price set on his head. Within the year he had gained sufficient foreign support to lead a small expedition back to his native land. That first venture failed but another which was more successful followed within a few months, then Bolívar took up the task of leadership of the patriot cause in the northern republics.

Within ten years the Spaniards were to be driven out of the entire continent.

During those years his power over the common people never failed him. The soldiers worshiped him and followed devotedly wherever he led. But with the other leaders in the wars he was not so successful. That was doubtless inevitable. The field of conflict was so wide. The jealousies were so great, and the desire for power of these men with their own followings so strong. Only at times could they sink their personal ambitions in a complete loyalty to any one chief. Nor was Bolívar always the man to command such loyalty. But in the great moments he did command it. His name will always be the great name in history, but from this time on there are other men who come into the picture with him, men whose stories we want to follow, for they, too, are "liberators."

PAEZ, THE MAN ON HORSEBACK

"From every blade of grass there seemed to spring a man and a horse!"

I T took every kind of South American, from the aristocratic creoles to the native Indians, descendants of the Incas, to win the long struggle for freedom from Spain; and Bolívar worked gladly with them all. To no group did he owe more in the years following his return from Jamaica than to the *llaneros*, cowboys, as they would have been called in our Far West, who lived on the grassy

—: 174 :—

plains that stretched from the base of the mountains along the great Venezuelan river valleys towards the sea. And to no leader did he owe more in those early days than to José Antonio Paez, who was often called "Paez the Centaur" because he was so constantly on horseback that it seemed as if he and his horse were one, like those mythical figures of ancient times which were said to be half man and half horse.

HIS BOYHOOD

Paez was not born a *llanero.* He was the son of a poor family in a hill village on the edge of the *llanos,* and fled as a boy to the plains for safety when he had killed a man who, according to his story, robbed him on the road and was on the point of murdering him. He was taken in at a cattle ranch and given employment by the negro overseer, a brutal giant who made the hard life doubly hard for this village boy who was so plainly above his calling. Perhaps this "Big Manuel," as he was called, took especial satisfaction in bullying young Paez and making him do menial tasks for him because the lad was so plainly of white blood, with blue eyes and wavy brown hair which contradicted the dark skin that was soon burned almost black by constant exposure to the tropical sun.

To know this early life of Paez and to picture the war as he and Bolívar carried it on in these first years of their campaigning, one must know these *llanos* of Venezuela, these vast grassy plains, trackless as our own western plains in pioneer days, but wholly different because they were in the tropics. Here roamed wild horses and cattle, descendants of the animals brought over three hundred years before by the conquistadores. Palms were the only trees in this great sea of waving grass which stretched as far as the eye could reach, and they were only in clumps which stood out like little islands or peninsulas in the great wide expanse. In the six months of the dry season the luxuriant grass grew high and the ground was baked and parched by the heat. Then the *llanero* longed only for cool water to slake his thirst and could not find it. But in the long rainy season the rivers and streams which wound through these acres overflowed, and the whole region became like a shallow inland sea through which the *llanero* splashed on his horse except when he came to the streams which he must swim or ford or when he was forced to take to a canoe. It was hot on the *llanos,* a dry burning heat or a moist sticky warmth, with the temperature rarely falling below the nineties. There was beauty here, with tropical birds nesting in the grasses and rare flowers springing up; and there was danger, with death-dealing alligators and electric eels lurking in the rivers.

When General Paez was an old man, he used to tell of his experiences in those days. Some of the boys were given half-tamed horses for their riding with the herds of cattle, and horses to guide and guard them, but Paez had always to break in wild colts for his bareback riding. He was doing his best to keep his seat on such an animal one day when the herd with which he was riding came to a swollen, turbulent stream which must be crossed. Big Manuel told him to swim across ahead of the animals, as was the custom when the frightened cattle must be driven through deep water.

"I cannot swim," the boy said miserably.

"I did not ask if you could swim," shouted the negro. "I said to jump into the river and guide the cattle to the other side."

Young Paez jumped in, and managed by clinging to his horse's mane through the dangerous passage to come through safely to the other shore, though there were moments on the way when he was nearly swept away.

It was a hard schooling, but Paez came through it to be the best *llanero* of the region, and an overseer himself on a small ranch by the time he was twenty-one. The fight for freedom had begun by this time, and he served with the patriot forces. From 1813 on he was taking a leading part in the guerrilla warfare, and went through a series of hairbreadth escapes from death, being held in prison in a royalist fort and led out more than once to be executed.

AS A FIGHTER

Many of the *llaneros* had begun their fighting under Boves on the royalist side, but after their leader's death they turned in the next campaigns to the patriot cause. General Morales, who succeeded Boves, tried to hold them, but the officers who came out from Spain had little use for these companies of wild-appearing men, who were of all breeds from Indian to white man. There is a tale of the time when Morales marshaled his five thousand *llaneros* for review by General Morillo, who had come out in charge of the king's big expedition and was fresh from the battlefields of Europe with the veterans of the Napoleonic wars.

"These are your victors," Morales announced; and the new commander gazed at the rough army in utter astonishment. The men from the plains were half-naked, many of them wearing only breech-clouts at the waist. They sat their small, half-wild horses carelessly and peered out under shocks of ill-kempt black hair at the gold-braided, uniformed general. They did not even know enough to salute, but held their long bamboo lances at any and every angle as the general rode past their lines.

"Here are the men who have won our victories," Morales declared again to the general.

"All of these men could be wiped out by a single one of my companies," General Morillo said scornfully.

But Morales knew better. He had seen these men fight, and when General Morillo insisted that this army be disciplined or disbanded, he gave the warning that if the general attempted either course, they would go over to the cause of the native patriots.

Events proved Morales right. When the warfare began again, the *llaneros* had found a new leader in Paez and were fighting on the patriot side. Tales of their victories came to Bolívar who had come back to Venezuela in 1816 from his Jamaican exile with a new plan of action. He had set up a headquarters on the banks of the Orinoco river, two hundred and fifty miles inland, to which supplies from abroad could come by water from the sea, and was seeking to unite the different fighting groups of the patriots in all the northern provinces. To this new capital, Angostura (called nowadays Ciudad Bolívar, or, as we should say, Bolívar City), there came one story of this new patriot leader far up in the *llanos* which pleased Bolívar exceedingly.

General Morillo's army, with three thousand men on foot and fifteen hundred on horseback, had marched out to defeat this *llanero* company which had been winning conspicuous victories over smaller forces. Paez had at that time only eleven hundred men with him, and defeat looked certain. But he used a plainsman's trick against the enemy. Many times in his life as cattle rancher Paez had protected himself and his herd from attacking wild animals by making a fire and walling his charges in by a defending wall of flame which reached to the bank of the nearest river. Now in the midst of the battle he noted which way the wind was blowing, and started such a fire in the direction of the attacking army. The royalists had been moving successfully on. All at once they found themselves marching towards a wall of flame which would have engulfed them if some of the officers had not discovered a stretch of swamp land to which they could escape.

There were stories, too, of the devotion of Paez's men, who adored this bluff, rough-and-ready fighter from their own ranks. He demanded and got instant obedience, but when the battles were over and the men were on the march, he would sit with them at their campfires and sing for hours the *llanero* songs with which they had herded their flocks through the long nights on the plains. "Cruel as a tiger," he was said to be in battle, but there was a story of his pardoning a brave fighter who had fallen into his hands and sending him up to the patriot headquarters with the advice that he change his allegiance and come over to the patriot side—which, indeed, the man did. "We are not assassins," Paez had said on that occasion. "After the victory we are always merciful." Bolívar, too, had turned from his old policy of "war-to-the-death" which had sent many helpless Spanish prisoners to the firing squads in the first campaign in Venezuela, and was practicing a less ruthless warfare.

MEETING WITH BOLÍVAR

Bolívar sent two of his colonels to ask Paez to come in under him, promising him full command of his own men if he would yield to his own authority as chief over all the forces. It is to Paez's credit that he accepted the offer. He knew that Bolívar had done great things for the Republic of Venezuela and in New Granada, and was well known abroad as well as at home. Besides, Bolívar was a highly educated man, while Paez could barely read or write. For all his dislike of having any man in authority over him, Paez knew that the Spanish armies were far more likely to be defeated if one man, and that man Bolívar, was in supreme control of the patriot forces. Had some of the

JOSÉ ANTONIO PAEZ
1790–1873

other leaders who were fighting for the rebel cause in different sections of the country been as willing as the *llanero* chief to come under a united command, the story of the next few years would have been very different. Moreover, Paez did not attempt to act without his men. Before he sent his answer back to Bolívar, he called in his own officers and convinced them of the wisdom of such action.

Both leaders started to come to their chosen place of meeting. Bolívar was moving up the Orinoco with an army of five thousand men, traveling the nine-hundred-mile course in the long, narrow dugouts of the native boatmen or on land along the banks. Paez had with him, besides a company of his *llanero* horsemen, several hundred naked Indians in war paraphernalia, armed with bows and arrows and wearing feathers on their heads.

They came together on a cattle farm, at the end of January, 1818. Paez was on horseback, as he always was, a stocky man, with big shoulders and chest and a large head, looking tall as he sat his horse, though when he got off he would be seen to be a short man with small legs that matched ill the upper part of his body. Bolívar was slender and graceful, sitting his horse with ease, his every movement full of health and vigor, his face alive with energy and dominated, as always, by his piercing black eyes. The two dismounted and embraced, in true Spanish-American fashion, and each complimented the other on his brilliant exploits and service to the patriot cause.

Side by side they stood the next day to review their strange assortment of troops, and together they marched northward. They came, after a period of marching, to the place on the Apure river, tributary of the Orinoco, where they wished to cross. There was a landing place on the far side of the river, and in the middle of the stream, which was a full quarter of a mile wide with a rapid current, there lay a squadron of armed launches belonging to the Spaniards. The patriots had no boats as yet, though some were being brought up-stream. For three or four days they waited, Bolívar holding back in the hope of the arrival of his boats, and Paez assuring him that he would provide the necessary boats if only the army would move.

At last they were camped within a mile of the river's edge, and Bolívar asked again where the promised boats were.

"There they are," said Paez, pointing to the launches in mid-stream.

"I see them," said Bolívar, "but what I do not see is how to take them."

"With our cavalry," replied Paez, smiling.

While Bolívar looked on, Paez and fifty of his "Guard of Honor," galloped to the bank, slid their saddles off and dashed without dismounting into the rapid stream, holding their lances in their mouths and guiding the animals by splashing water in their faces. The *llaneros* on the shore kept up a constant yelling to frighten alligators away, and succeeded by so doing, in confusing the Spaniards so that they took to their canoes and fled. The *llaneros* leaped from their horses' backs to the decks of the boats, turned their horses loose to swim back to the shore, and guided the vessels to the bank where Bolívar and his staff stood watching. Paez had won his first victory for Bolívar.

LATER LIFE

There were to be other victories which the two men won together, and defeats which they suffered. Paez was at one time called sharply to account by his chief for his independent acts and the insistence on his own ways of waging war. He was to have a political career at the close of the wars, in which he finally took sides against Bolívar and became the president of Venezuela when that country separated from the great northern super-state which Bolívar endeavored to establish.* He was a broad-minded ruler, granting religious freedom but giving state support to the Catholic church, and helping trade. He put down revolts, reduced the army, and passed measures favorable to the Indians. But he suffered party defeat and withdrew to the United States, living in New York after a visit to the capitals of Europe, where the former *llanero* was richly entertained. He wrote there his autobiography before he died in 1873. But the memory of the man that has lasted down the years is of the fighting chieftain, the man on horseback. Two stories have come down to us which give us that picture.

In one of his battles with the Spaniards his favorite

* See page 197.

horse was shot beneath him. The general wept as he rose from the ground to which he had been thrown and gazed at the dying animal. Then he leaped out ahead of his *llaneros* and shouted:

"Men! over there are the Spaniards! They have just killed my horse. I am going to avenge him. . . . Men, are you with me? Will you follow me? Will you avenge that horse of mine?"

With one voice the wild men of the plains shouted back:

"Yes, Chief. We will avenge your horse!"

"Then charge!" yelled their leader, and they drove madly against the enemy, brandishing their lances.

The royalists did not know that their defeat that day was due to a single chance shot that killed a horse.

The other story is kept in mind by a statue of the general in the city of Caracas. In a battle with Morillo's men the patriots seemed hopelessly outnumbered, and retreat was the only possibility. The flight was in full swing, with the royalist soldiers charging confidently across the field. But General Paez and his hundred and fifty best men were in the rear of the patriot forces, seeming to flee as rapidly as their horses would take them. Suddenly Paez shouted "Turn your faces," and the men swung around their horses and charged straight into the ranks of their pursuers and completely routed them. Thomas Ybarra, Venezuelan historian, describes that statue as "of a rider reining in a magnificent charger, so suddenly as to bring it to its hind legs and make it throw back its head at the sudden thrust of the bit between its teeth, while he, wild-eyed, hair streaming in the wind, shakes over his head a lance and, face turned over his shoulder and mouth opened wide, is apparently uttering some ringing word of command." That is how South America likes to remember General José Antonio Paez as he was in his years as Bolívar's devoted associate and able general, rather than in the later period of his political activity. Here he embodies the spirit of a free country.

THE LIBERATOR IN ACTION

"The indefatigable Bolívar, whose extraordinary exertions for the emancipation of his country have, by the unanimous voice of America and Europe, justly entitled him to the illustrious appellation of 'the Washington of South America.'"—Henry Clay

QUICK pictures of Simón Bolívar are all that we can give for the next few years. Yet perhaps for a man whose life was made up of dramatic episodes and surprise appearances, such pictures give as good a portrait as the longer stories. At least we can try to see him as the handful of devoted followers who were always with him saw him during the fighting years from 1818 to 1824. Those were the years in which he was freeing the territories which were to become the three northern republics of South America, Venezuela, Colombia, and Ecuador, and then going south to complete the freeing of Peru and for the establishment of the new republic which was to be named for him, Bolivia. Into those years he crowded what another man might have taken half a lifetime to accomplish.

"EVEN TO CAPE HORN"

We can see him first as his opponents saw him. General Morillo, one of the most experienced officers of the Spanish army, came out to South America at the close of the Napoleonic wars with an army of fifteen thousand veteran soldiers, newly released by Napoleon's defeat from the battlefields of Europe. King Ferdinand VII had been delivered from prison and was back on the throne of Spain, restoring the severe rule and the overbearing despotism that had been eased and modified during the time of the Regency which acted in his stead. He was impatient at the news of disorder and rebellion in his colonies, and sent Morillo out with definite orders. He was to begin at the northern coast and march southward to Buenos Aires, bringing all the Spanish-American colonies back under royal control *within the space of one hundred and sixty days*. Morillo had come out in 1815. It was now 1818, and he and his army had not been able to conquer the northern regions of Venezuela and New Granada (now Colombia), nor to leave them behind and go south, because of what he would have called the annoying, guerrilla warfare of those rebel soldiers, Bolívar, Paez, the *llanero* chieftain, and Santander of New Granada. But during the year 1818 it looked as though he might be going to succeed.

Morillo could not understand why he had not succeeded. The patriot forces under Bolívar suffered during that year a series of heart-breaking defeats. Even General Paez was moved by Bolívar's constant returning to battle in spite of losses, to say that his leader was "overfond of fighting"; and that was a great deal for a man to say who loved a good fight as well as did the *llanero*. Morillo could not understand the persistence of his opponent. Our picture comes from the report he wrote home to the king. "Twelve consecutive battles," he said, "in which his best troops and officers have been killed on the field, have not been sufficient to break his self-confidence nor the tenacity with which he makes war against us." That was Bolívar. He did not let himself know that he was defeated; and in his mind, in spite of the defeats and losses, he was accomplishing two objects which he had set as his goals that year. He was keeping the Spanish forces occupied in the north, and he was delaying other action because he hoped to get help from outside. The Spanish veterans were not the only soldiers released by the close of the Napoleonic wars. There were British soldiers whom Bolívar's friend and associate, Mendez, who had gone to London with him in 1810 and stayed on in Miranda's house to work for the cause, was signing up for the South American fight. British and North American sentiment were swinging his way, and the officers and men who were beginning to arrive from London were experienced soldiers who were to be a great help.

Our next picture of Bolívar might well be of him as a legislator, calling together a congress to govern the new republic of Venezuela, which he was re-establishing with its capital at Angostura on the Orinoco river instead of north at Caracas, where the other republics had centered. We might see him writing day and night on the constitution for the new country, and meeting with his legislators. But that work was soon over, and he was restless for the

next move. The announcement of his plan came one evening at a banquet which he was giving for Mr. Irvine, the
American commercial agent whom he liked to call the
"American ambassador." Like Miranda, Bolívar was always looking to the United States for aid.

At this big dinner the talk about American independence became more and more eager and excited. Just as
dessert was served, in the middle of one of his own sentences, Bolívar rose impetuously, jumped on the table's top,
and strode down its length and back, amid the clatter of
breaking glass and falling china, exclaiming: "Even so I
shall march from the Atlantic to the Pacific, from Panama
to Cape Horn, until the last Spaniard is expelled!" Some
of his guests looked on embarrassed and startled, thinking the man mad, but not so his fellow-officers. This was
the Bolívar they adored. They would follow him to the
world's end.

There was another such moment a few months later,
but not in a banquet hall. This conference took place in
an empty mud hut in a tiny village far out on the grassy
plains that stretched along the banks of the rivers. On his
way to this conference Bolívar had had to stop and deal
firmly with his associate, General Paez, the *llanero* chieftain of all this vast territory, who had been getting too
independent in his plans for campaigns and needed to be
brought back to his first loyalty. Bolívar had succeeded.
Paez had promised complete coöperation from his *llaneros*.
He had done more, for on the heels of the interview there

came a battle with Morillo's army in which Paez seemed to retreat for the moment and then shouted his celebrated command, "Turn faces," and routed this enemy which so outnumbered his tiny forces.

Bolívar sent out the word for his officers to meet him at the little village in the heart of the great plains, and they came. They sat on the floor or on the dried, sun-bleached skulls of cattle which served as stools, while their black-haired, slender leader walked up and down, talking and gesticulating. General Daniel O'Leary, who had come out from Ireland and become his close companion and secretary, describes him at this time, and it is worth while for us to stop a moment and get the picture clear again.

> Bolívar had a high but not very wide forehead, wrinkled from an early age; the mark of a thinker. Heavy and well-formed eyebrows. Black eyes, alert and penetrating. Nose long and perfect . . . mouth ugly and the lips rather thick. . . . Teeth white, uniform and beautiful; he took excellent care of them. His ears were large but well placed. Hair black, fine and curly . . . side whiskers and mustache reddish . . . chest narrow, body slender, especially the legs . . . skin dark and somewhat rough . . . hands and feet small and well-formed. . . . He took much exercise. I have never known anybody that endured fatigue like him.

It was not a cheerful story that Bolívar had to tell his officers. Morillo had seventeen thousand men in Venezuela, Bolívar and Paez less than seven thousand. There could be attacks and counter-attacks out on the plains and in the river valleys, where the native troops could hold off the Spanish warriors for the time. But—and Bolívar's face must have begun to light up as he talked—over in New Granada there were not nearly so many Spaniards, and they were scattered over the whole province. Santander, the patriot leader, was there, with a small force of his own. What would they say to having their army join his so that together they could give battle to the enemy?

The men listened, and then began to show astonishment as they gradually took in the idea. New Granada was on the other side of the continent. Between these plains where they were now meeting and New Granada lay hundreds of miles of *llanos* crossed by rapid rivers. It was now the rainy season, and that territory would be almost impassable for an army. But the plains were as nothing to what lay beyond. They stretched to the eastward slope of the great mountain range of the Andes. Beyond them those mountains towered like an impassable wall between the Venezuelan plains and New Granada. After the earthquake at Caracas in 1812, Bolívar had made the remark, never to be forgotten, "If Nature opposes us, we will battle with her, too, and compel her to obey us!" Now it was as if he were saying it again, with this mountain barrier in mind.

The men argued hotly. The cavalry leader declared that it could not be done. Not a man or horse could make the trip over those heights. Others questioned and shook their heads. It was impossible, a fantastic idea. Bolívar listened unmoved. "We shall cross the Andes," he said; and all at

—: 191 :—

once one of his British volunteers, Rooke, a gallant Irishman, leaped to his feet.

"General Bolívar, lead the way," he cried. "Say the word and I'll march with you not only over the Andes but right down to Patagonia—even to Cape Horn!"

Swung by his enthusiasm and Bolívar's steady purpose, the others agreed. On May 26, 1819, the march began.

OVER THE ANDES

No man but Bolívar would have dreamed of that march, nor been able to lead his men through it. Thirteen hundred men on foot, eight hundred on horses started out. But they were not the marching army which those words might well call up as a picture. They were a moving horde, poorly disciplined, ill-clad, and poorly armed. They drove cattle along with them for food, as they started over the *llanos* in this rainy season of the year, with rivers to ford and seas of wet grassland to navigate.

For one week the march across the flooded *llanos* went on, with men lost in the rushing rivers as they attempted to ford them, with cattle lost, and clothes becoming damp rags in the tropical heat and humidity. All these days Bolívar rode up and down the long line on his horse, encouraging men who faltered, lifting those who fell, snatching a man from the river as he was attacked by a devouring alligator, always pressing on.

Then the country changed. The army moved up the first slopes of the mountains, and the cold winds swept down on those men of the plains who had never before been off their low, grassy lands and were now almost naked after the wet march behind them. They felt the dreaded mountain sickness which caught their lungs so that they could not breathe, and gave them nausea and a numbing pain in the head and limbs so that they could hardly move. Many fell from the narrow mountain paths and their bodies crashed into the chasms below. Horses lay down to die, but men kept on, beating their freezing hands and faces. The Irishman Rooke tried to keep up their spirits with talk of how he had heard that this mountain climate was said to be the finest in the world, and they laughed at his jests and plodded on in the midst of their pain.

At one of the mountain passes they came upon a small guard of the enemy, seven hundred Spaniards, who seemed to the wearied men to be twice that number. But they pushed them back, with Bolívar leading the attack. The Spaniards were retreating to a safer place for their stand, expecting to meet this invading force again. But Bolívar had another plan, made necessary by this encounter and by the news thus gained of the larger army guarding what was believed to be the only road across the mountains. It was the only *road,* but not the only *route.*

"Tonight we shall go over the Paramo," Bolívar told his exhausted soldiers.

The council of officers listened and could hardly believe their ears. The Paramo de Pisba was a mountain plateau, high up in these incredibly high mountains, where freezing winds always blew and neither man nor beast nor growing plant could live in the eternal snow.

That night they made the desperate journey, with icy rain freezing on such garments as they still had, with faces and hands and feet freezing if they stopped beating them, with no food, and no chance to lie down and rest for a moment lest they freeze. Many did drop and die. But the others pushed on, and at dawn Bolívar stood at the head of the line and shook the hand of each survivor as he stumbled past him, telling them that the impossible had been accomplished, that they were heroes for their cause.

Of the two thousand who had started weeks before, hundreds had died on the long march. But the strongest survived. They could not linger long in the lovely green valley where the astonished inhabitants welcomed and sheltered and fed them. They knew that they must press on to attack the Spanish army which was guarding the roads against them, and then go forward to deliver the capital of New Granada, the city of Bogotá, from the Spanish rule by which it had been so long oppressed.

The plans were made; horses and arms were gathered; preparations were going on well; and the men seemed to be recovering from their ordeal. But Rooke noticed one day that the Liberator was walking by himself, with an expression of sadness on his face. What was disturbing him, he asked, when he had just accomplished the greatest march for independence in history?

"I am thinking," replied Bolívar, "of those we left up there, of the hundreds of brave men we have lost."

More were to be lost in the next engagements. In a

fight with the advancing Spanish forces Rooke himself was seriously wounded, and died after the amputation of his arm. He died gallantly, as he had lived. At the last he murmured, "Long live my country!" When they asked which country he meant, England or Ireland, he said faintly, "To the country about to give me a grave!"

At the Battle of Boyacá, a few days later, Bolívar and his armies won a smashing victory, not only defeating the Spanish forces but taking nearly two thousand prisoners. This is one of the leading battles of the Wars of Independence. It stands as the victory which freed New Granada.

News of the defeat came to Bogotá, and the viceroy fled in terror, forgetting in his haste either to empty or lock up the royal treasury. The citizens, wild with delight, streamed out along the road to Boyaca, strewing it with flowers over which the conquering heroes should walk. The soldiers were dirty, ill-clad, barefoot, but men, women, and children embraced them and covered their rags with garlands of flowers.

The other generals came, among them the Bogotá hero, Santander, who had worked for two years towards this victory. But all eyes turned to Bolívar. He sat on his horse, smiling, shaking the hands which were reached up to him. At the palace he dismounted and ran up the steps, where the chief citizens of the newly freed city were waiting to receive him. An onlooker reports that Bolívar was wearing a black dress coat, white trousers, cavalry boots, and a helmet of rawhide. He, too, was fresh from the battlefield and without his usual fine uniform with its many buttons, medals, and gold stripes.

A new government was soon set up, and the citizens declared that "The President and General of the Armies of the Republic, Simón Bolívar, is the Liberator of New Granada." Santander was one of those who shared his honors on the public day of celebration when Bolívar was given the title and the crown of laurel to mark his triumph.

A MEETING WITH MORILLO
1820

By his conquest of the greater portion of New Granada, Bolívar cut the South American empire of Spain in halves. In the north Morillo and his armies still held Caracas and the better part of Venezuela, though Bolívar's capital at Angostura, and the river valleys to the south and west, and the vast plains were in patriot hands. New Granada was rich, fertile territory, with much man-power for Bolívar's future campaigns.

With victory came Bolívar's troubles with his associates. Each leader was eager for authority, and the loyalty to the Liberator was sure only on the battlefield. When he was away from any region, those in charge took matters in their own hands. He left Santander in charge at Bogotá, as Vice President of the Republic, and was greatly disturbed when Santander used his authority to put to death Barreiro, commander of the Spanish troops at Boyacá, and thirty-eight of his officers, with the reason or excuse that there might be an uprising in their favor. Bolívar returned to Angostura to find his subordinates there plotting against his rule in Venezuela. As was usual in these cases, Bolívar's presence put an end to the trouble for the time. His strong personality could always win back those whom he met face to face. But the troubles that were to make his career difficult were under way even in these times of his triumph.

Bolívar took this occasion to put into effect his new plan of government. He created, with the consent of the assembly, a great new State, Colombia, which was not simply the republic of today that bears that name, but a much greater republic embracing Venezuela, New Granada, and Quito (now Ecuador) on the Pacific, which he had not even conquered. Of this new Republic he was President, with men for each region as Vice Presidents.

The stage was set now for a fight with Morillo and his men. But once more, as in the time of the invasion of Spain by Napoleon, events in the Old World played a part in events in the New World. Morillo had been greatly cheered by receiving word that King Ferdinand was planning to send a great expedition, far greater than the one with which he had come in 1815, to subdue once and for all the rebellious colonies. The same news coming to Buenos Aires threatened an end to the hopes of General San Martín for getting any help for his expedition to free Peru. When the news came to Morillo, he saw to it that Bolívar heard of it promptly. Such a plan was a serious threat to the Liberator's growing power.

But on the heels of that information came another report. There was mutiny in some of the companies in the Spanish army. A revolt had set in against the king's despotic rule, and he must heed it. Besides, there was yellow fever in the army. Fortunately for the cause of South American independence, both in Argentina and Chile and in the north, that expedition never started.

Instead, King Ferdinand granted to his subjects at home a new and far more liberal constitution than the old one, and ordered Morillo to announce to the colonists the granting of this new constitution and to negotiate with Bolívar with a view to a possible peace treaty.

To say that Morillo was angry is to put it mildly.

"They are fools in Madrid," he said to his fellow officers. "The king knows nothing of the happenings here. This is worse than humiliating. It is degrading. . . . And how it will amuse Bolívar!"

It did amuse Bolívar, and please him, too. He began a correspondence with the General in which he agreed to negotiate provided Colombia was recognized as an independent republic; and he signed his name with the title of "President of Colombia." Morillo replied refusing to recognize the existence of the republic, much less its independence. For a time the deadlock continued, but at last the issue was ignored and commissioners representing the two leaders arranged a six-months' armistice. Then the surprising thing happened. Morillo expressed a desire to meet the young creole leader whom he was fighting, and Bolívar was curious to meet the Spanish commander.

The date was set, the meeting-place to be at Santa Ana, halfway between the two armies. Morillo, in his fine uniform, arrived on November 27, 1820, with a staff of fifty officers. Soon O'Leary rode up, announcing the coming of Bolívar. Finding that the patriot leader had only ten or a dozen staff officers with him, Morillo dismissed his cavalry squadron, keeping only his few officers with him.

"Bolívar has outdone me in generosity," he said, as he gave the orders to the men to ride back to headquarters.

They rode forward and saw a group of horsemen coming.

"Which one is Bolívar?" Morillo inquired, and O'Leary pointed him out.

"What, that little man with the blue coat and cap, riding a mule?" he said.

The two parties met, and Bolívar and Morillo leaped from their saddles and embraced. It was a tiny village to which they had come, with only huts for their shelter. The two leaders went to one hut and breakfasted together, while their officers fraternized cordially in another hut. All day the two men talked together, and they slept under the same roof after their banquet that night. Years before, Morillo had written of Bolívar to his king: "Nothing can compare with the untiring activity of that leader. His fearlessness and his talents entitle him to his place at the head of the revolution and of the war; but he possesses as well, from his noble Spanish strain, and his education, also Spanish, qualities of elegance and generosity which elevate him far above all which surround him. He *is* the revolution." As the hours of conversation went by, that feeling must have grown stronger. Morillo wrote later to a friend that this was one of the happiest days of his life. "It was like a dream," he said, "to see ourselves united there as Spaniards, brothers, and friends."

When the two must separate the following morning, the Spanish commander suggested that a monument should be erected at that spot to commemorate the meeting. Soldiers who were standing by pushed a big boulder into place, and the two men clasped hands over it, expressing once more their wish that lasting peace might soon come.

They rode away, never to meet again, for Morillo was soon recalled to Spain, and another veteran soldier, La Torree, came out in his place.

MORE TRIUMPHS

The armistice did not last the full six months for which it was intended. In the spring of 1821 the two armies were fighting again, and on June 24th Bolívar won his second great, decisive battle. At Boyacá in 1819 he had gained the freedom of New Granada. Now on the plains of Carabobo, in Venezuela, he and his men routed completely the Spanish army and established the permanent independence of Venezuela. Five days later he entered again the city of Caracas, which he had entered so many years before at the beginning of the revolution. But this time the victory was complete and final. The north was won.

Now Bolívar's thoughts turned southward to Quito (the modern Ecuador), which he had always counted as part

BOLÍVAR, LIBERATOR OF FIVE NATIONS

of his great northern republic which he was calling Colombia. Young General Sucre had been sent down in advance to deliver that region, and he had been making his way with difficult fighting. A year after the Battle of Carabobo, Sucre was in the city of Quito, and it remained only for Bolívar to join him and complete the adoption of this people into the great patriot republic. The year had not been a happy one for Bolívar. There were jealousies among the leaders that had led Bolívar to write to a friend the truth which was to be sadly proved in the final years of his life, "I fear peace even more than I fear war." But he had left behind the dissensions at Bogotá and marched with his army southward through a region which presented almost as many difficulties as the famous march over the Andes. There are pictures of him as the defiant warrior. He came in his march along a mountain river bank to a place where sheer walls of rock seemed to make his advance impossible—and there a Spanish army awaited him. "The position is formidable," he said to his officers. "But we cannot remain here, nor can we retreat. We must conquer and we will." At last he took the stubbornly defended city of Pasto and was ready to march on to complete the conquest by joining General Sucre in the capital city of Quito. The final triumph came with Bolívar's entrance into Quito, where the city went wild in their joy at his coming and its leading citizens expressed the desire to have the entire province become a part of the larger Colombia.

Six weeks later Bolívar met San Martín at Guayaquil,

the port of the region, and the two discussed together the future of the struggle in Peru. The story of that meeting has already been told in the chapter on San Martín.* The "Protector of Peru" had hoped that Bolívar would send in troops to complete with him the conquest, but it became plain that the two could not carry on together. Bolívar must be left to act alone and in his own way. San Martín withdrew, and a year later Bolívar went into Peru, at the invitation of its leaders, to help them in the final task of driving the Spanish forces out.

A description of Bolívar at this time helps us to understand the effect which his presence had on his fellow-countrymen.

> The gift of speaking with facility and promptness possessed by the Liberator, was wonderful, [says Larrazabal] he being most happy in the art of collecting his ideas rapidly. His soul mounted quickly to the serene heights of thought and thence overflowed in torrents of eloquence. . . . He spoke on campaigns, in the palace, at the entrance to the cities where hundreds of persons sallied to meet him; wherever it was essential to sow the seed of American liberty, there his speech broke forth like a prodigy.

At the close of the banquet given in honor of his coming, General O'Higgins of Chile, who was a guest, shouted, "Bolívar is the greatest man in South America."

The pictures of Bolívar in these times when he was campaigning, organizing armies, settling the affairs of newly adopted regions, and directing at a distance his busi-

* See page 104.

ness as President of Colombia, are of a man of tremendous, nervous driving power. He could keep three secretaries busy at once, and none could be found who was swift enough for him. He complained once that he wore one out in three days, and then there must be a search for another. The campaign against the Spanish forces in Peru was as difficult as any that Bolívar had ever undertaken. Once more he had to create an army, gather supplies, fight and plan and fight again. Much of the time he was ill, with a fever that threatened at one time his life, but from a hammock in a garden where a friend found him lying, too weak even to sit up to welcome him, he said in reply to a question as to what he could do now, in a particularly dark hour in the war, "Do? Why, conquer, of course!"

In December, 1824, General Sucre fought at Ayacucho the most famous and final battle of the Wars of Independence, ending the Spanish control of South America. There were honors all along the way for Bolívar now. In Lima, Peru, they had made him Dictator, and hung under his portrait the inscription, "He created Colombia, restored Peru, gave peace to America." He entered the ancient city of Cuzco, the long-ago capital where Pizarro had met the Inca emperor three hundred years before. When Sucre had come to the city, he had found there Pizarro's banner, and had sent it to Bolívar as "a trophy worthy of the warrior who showed the Colombian army the road to glory and to the liberation of Peru."

From Cuzco Bolívar went on into southern Peru, and

joined with Sucre in the creation of the new state which was to bear his name. At the city of La Paz in the new Bolivia, he was given a splendid welcome, and presented with golden trappings for his horse, gold spurs, and a crown of gold and precious stones. They knew how to honor conquering heroes in South America in those days. But Bolívar knew his part, too. He passed these treasures over to General Sucre, who in turn passed them on to those who had helped him to win the victory.

DREAMER AND PROPHET

*"All who have served the Revolution
have ploughed the sea."*—Bolívar

READING of Bolívar's triumphs, one wishes that
the story could have ended there. But that is for
his sake rather than for that of the world. The few remaining years of his life were to be filled with tragic disappointments. Yet all the while he was dreaming the
dreams which show him to have been far ahead of his
time.

From the days of the Jamaica Letter, when in exile he
talked of the future of the whole of South America as if
it were already accomplished, Bolívar had looked to the
unity of all the new governments as his goal. He did not
believe in a federation there, as many of his fellow-patriots
did. He wanted a great state, a republic with the unity of
the Spanish empire with separate parts, and he set himself
first to make such a state out of Venezuela, New Granada,
Quito, hoping that it would point the way and be joined
by southern states. That endeavor failed utterly, and its
failure broke Bolívar's heart and sent him once more into
exile.

But Bolívar's dreams did not stop with South America.
In 1822, Henry Clay had succeeded in getting the United

States government to recognize Bolívar's republic as an independent nation. This was a great step, for it put the seal of recognition on Bolívar's accomplishments. Bolívar was never a local person. The letters which he wrote with such speed in camps, huts, palaces, wherever he happened to be, went out to friends all over the world. His fame was greater in Europe than in his own land, and in the United States he was honored as a second Washington.

PAN-AMERICA

While he ruled as dictator in Peru, in 1824, Bolívar began to take definite steps to fulfill another dream of union. In 1823 President Monroe in his annual message to Congress on December second had put forth the "doctrine" which was to be known by his name, warning European nations that interference with the destinies of any of the independent governments, now established, on the American continents would be looked upon with disfavor by the United States. Bolívar had begun as early as 1815 to think of the union which should come when the Spanish-American empire fell to pieces. In 1822, as President of Colombia, he had suggested that the new Spanish-American nations prepare for a conference at Panama. From Peru in December, 1824, he issued invitations to these states to attend such a conference in the summer of 1826. He did not invite the United States, partly perhaps because he was anxious to end slavery in South America and feared the influence of so strong a slaveholding nation on the deliberations on that point. Vice President Santander of Colombia added, however, invitations to the United States, Great Britain, and Brazil.

The dream was, however, Bolívar's. Looking forward to the day of meeting he said: "The day in which our plenipotentiaries exchange their credentials, will fix an immortal epoch in the diplomatic history of America. When, after a hundred years, posterity shall seek the origin of our public law and recall the compacts which have consolidated our destiny, it will remember with respect the protocols of our Isthmus. In them will be found the basis of the first alliances which will trace the march of our relations with the world."

Long debates in the United States Congress delayed the start of our own two delegates so that they did not arrive in Panama until the first session of the Panama Congress had ended. A second session, called to meet shortly in Mexico, was never held. Only four states were represented at the first Congress—Mexico, Central America, Colombia, and Peru. They arranged for certain treaties of union and arbitration between their own governments and any others which would join.

Bolívar's dream of a "united America, worthy of being called the Queen of Nations, the Mother of Republics," has not succeeded. His dream of a court of international law and a central body of men for arbitration of differences has not yet come true. Yet what a vision it was, in those early years of the nineteenth century, for a young South American to look on the Americas—and the world—as he did, and say:

If the world were to select a spot for its capital, it would seem that the Isthmus of Panama must needs be chosen for this august dignity, situated as it is in the center of the world, looking in one direction towards Asia, in the other towards Africa and Europe, and equidistant from America's two extremities.

The failure of the conference to accomplish anything was one of the disappointments which came to Bolívar as he struggled with the problems of Peru and his disunited Republic of Colombia in 1826.

PANAMA CANAL

One other forward look should be credited to Bolívar. He saw the possibility of a canal across the Isthmus of Panama, and sent engineers to study the ground and decide where it might well be cut. His time was too short. There was neither time nor money nor inclination for such a project in the brief days of his power. But the vision of the man must always be remembered in these later days when his dreams have to a certain extent come true.

IN THE LAST DAYS

"I have freed the New World but you cannot say that I have perfected the stability or happiness of one of the nations which compose it."—Bolívar to Sucre.

BOLÍVAR did well to fear the days of peace more than those of war. In the years following the expulsion of the Spaniards from control of South America, he had to see his former friends rise up against him, Santander in Colombia, and at the last, Paez in Venezuela. He was accused of wishing to make himself king. He did not get on well with the legislative bodies which he had created. His reforms were too rapid. His love of titles and power was probably too great. He offered again and again to resign his high offices, but still he held them, with the idea which was sometimes all too true that he was the only man who had a chance of success in leadership. There was talk among the political circles of setting up once more some kind of a monarchy to rule the freed colonies, and Bolívar was appalled, and went about the business of opposing it steadfastly, and in his fear of such measures, he made the mistake of setting himself up as a dictator.

There are bright pictures during these years. The family of President Washington, admiring Bolívar and his achievements, desired to send to him a gold medal, presented to Washington by the United States, with also a small locket containing a miniature of the President and a lock of his hair. They asked Lafayette, then on a farewell visit to the United States, to represent them in the matter, and he dispatched the package with a letter on September 1, 1825. On the back of the locket had been inscribed Latin words which, translated, said: "This portrait of the Liberator of North America is presented by his adopted son to him who achieved similar glory in South America." The gift was from George Washington Custis, representing the family. The letter from Lafayette said: "I feel that, of all living men and of all men in history, my friend General Washington would not have preferred any to yourself as the recipient of this gift. What more can I say to the great citizen whom South America hails with the title of Liberator, a title confirmed by both hemispheres—a man who bears in his heart an unlimited love for liberty and an absolutely pure love for republicanism?"

Bolívar was always devoted to his own family and to those who had cared for him in his youth. In Peru he received a letter from his sister in Caracas telling that Hipólita, his negro nurse in his childhood, was in need. "See that she gets whatever she asks for," he wrote back quickly. "Hipólita gave me the milk that nourished me as a child. She was, to this orphan, both father and mother. Let her want for nothing."

His old tutor, Rodriguez, turned up at this time, and Bolívar welcomed him gladly and gave him a position

Courtesy Pan-American Union

STATUE OF SIMÓN BOLÍVAR IN CARTAGENA, COLOMBIA

of authority as "Director of Education" in Bolivia, where the old man nearly drove President Sucre mad with his wild theories until he finally departed in disgust. But Bolívar had been overjoyed to see his old-time friend.

There were always women in Bolívar's life. Since 1822 a brilliant and attractive lady, Manuela Saenz, had been often with him, presiding at his table and being accepted by officers and guests. In 1828 the break between him and Santander had become open, and Bogotá was a center of plots and counter-plots against the Liberator. Hints of a plan for his assassination reached Bolívar, and he tried to have it tracked down, but gave the order apparently to one of the conspirators, who warned his friends that they must act quickly if they were to act at all.

On a September night in 1828 they attacked the palace at Bogotá where the President was sleeping, killed the guards, and hurried to the room where they expected to find him. He had been there, but Manuela, hearing the disturbance, had roused him and begged him to flee. "There are too many of them," she said. "Jump out the window." Bolívar dropped to the pavement below, and was barely gone when the heavy knocking came at the door. Manuela met the men calmly and said, "The Liberator is not here." They pressed her, and she repeated her words; "He is not here." "Where is he?" they questioned. "At the Council Hall," she replied quietly.

They shut Manuela in a closet and went out into the streets to find him. Hearing the sounds of fighting, he fled from the palace. Not knowing who was friend or foe, he could not appear on the streets, but crawled through the garden to a ravine beyond the palace. At its foot was a stream over which there was a bridge. In his night-shirt he stood all night in the icy-cold water, while the sounds of tumult in the palace and the streets came to him. Manuela was found and released, and she and his friends among the officers searched the town as daylight approached, shouting his name.

"General Bolívar, where are you?" they called. "We are your friends. Come out to us."

At last he became convinced that he recognized voices he knew, and came out. His friends greeted him with mad joy, for they had almost given him up as dead. As they went to the palace, shouts came from the hundreds of people gathered in the streets, "Viva el Libertador!" The news had spread that Bolívar was safe. Bolívar turned to Manuela. She, he said, was the "liberatress" of the Liberator.

The conspirators were promptly punished. Santander, who denied any knowledge of the plot, was suspected because of his known enmity to Bolívar and sent into exile. But the trouble did not end. Civil war followed, Venezuela under Paez seceded from the union, and Quito was ready to follow. The enmity was turned against him, and he despaired of conquering it. The Liberator was ill, suffering torture from fever and rheumatism. He had driven himself too hard, and now the will to live was leaving him as he saw the horrors of civil war and vicious politics in the lands he had freed.

In 1829 and again in 1830 he handed to the Congress of Colombia his resignation as President of the Republic, and at last they accepted it, seeing that it was his wish in this unhappy state of affairs. He left Bogotá without any money, for he had lost his private fortune at the hands of Monteverde at the beginning of the Wars of Independence and had never enriched himself out of the public treasury. Now that he intended to depart for foreign lands, he had hardly anything with which to pay his way. The Congress had voted him a pension, but there was no money to pay it.

A last blow came to him. Sucre, who had been to him like a son, was assassinated. Bolívar was desperately ill at the time. When the word came to him, he gasped: "Good God! they have killed Abel!"

He desired now only to get away, but he was too ill. When the heat became intolerable, he was moved to his country home. In November he was gotten aboard a brigantine bound for Jamaica, but the sea voyage from which his friends had hoped for benefit to his health was more than he could stand. On the first of December, 1830, he was carried ashore in a chair to Santa Marta, in northeastern Colombia, where friends awaited him. A French doctor ministered to him, but it was too late. He knew he was going and made his preparations, receiving the last sacrament of the church, and preparing a last proclamation to his fellow-countrymen.

"Colombians!" it said in its concluding words, "My last wishes are for the felicity of the *patria*. If my death contributes to the breaking down of parties and the union is consolidated, I shall go down in peace into the grave."

On December 17, 1830, Simón Bolívar died, at the age of forty-seven years. With the passage of time there has come to his fellow-countrymen and the world an appreciation of his true greatness. In measures which concerned the common people he was progressive, desiring freedom for the slaves, furthering education, and urging democratic institutions. He had the faults which matched his virtues, but he had also the long vision and the world outlook of the statesman.

TWO NORTHERN PATRIOTS

SUCRE
SANTANDER

GENERAL SUCRE

"General Sucre is the hero of Ayacucho; he is the redeemer of the Children of the Sun. He has broken the chains with which Pizarro bound the empire of the Incas."—Bolívar.

IN an All-America roll call of honor no name is more welcome or more worthy than that of Antonio Sucre, who is too little known beyond the bounds of Bolivia, which, with his chief Bolívar, he founded, and the northern republics where he fought bravely and with distinction from the beginning of the revolution. We find frequent mention of him in every biography of Bolívar, and are so attracted to the man that we must track down his own story and see him alone, with the special charm that is his. Sucre is a leader whom any nation would delight to honor. His contribution to the story of the Americas is one that is the rightful inheritance of every American, whether of the northern continent or the southern.

HIS FAMILY STORY

This boy who was destined to win the final battle which drove the Spaniards forever from South America, Antonio José de Sucre, was born on February 3, 1795, in Cumana in the eastern part of Venezuela. He came of a distinguished line of ancestors on both sides. On the side of his mother, Dona Maria Manuela del Alcalá, he could trace back three hundred years to the conquistadores, who conquered and explored all this northern region. On his father's side were feudal lords who served the House of Burgundy during the fifteenth century and later in Europe. One member of the family, born in Flanders, came to America at the beginning of the eighteenth century and became in 1715 Governor of Santiago de Cuba. Antonio's father, Vicénte de Sucre, was a lieutenant in the Spanish army until the beginning of the revolution in Caracas in 1810, when he and Antonio's uncle cast in their lot with the patriots.

Antonio was only fifteen years old at this time. His mother had died when he was a child. His schooling had

ANTONIO JOSÉ DE SUCRE
1795–1830
After Felix Acevedo.

been limited until the fortunate time when he had the chance to study under the colonel of engineers at Cumana. From him he learned the mathematics and the principles of fortifications which were to be so valuable to him in later years. When he came to Bolívar, the Liberator commented to his secretary, O'Leary, that Sucre was one of the best officers in the army, combining professional learning with brains, activity, and a kind disposition.

At the age of seventeen young Sucre was given the privilege of a place on General Miranda's staff; and it is pleasant to know that in the midst of the criticisms of that unhappy time, he was loyal to his chief to the end. The failure of the revolution sent forty-five of the young patriot soldiers into exile in the English West Indies, where Sucre had a chance to complete his education, studying English and American history and becoming familiar with the political movements in Europe. In 1813 he was back in Venezuela, fighting under Marino, who was liberating the eastern section of the country while Bolívar was coming over from New Granada to free the western portion. Sucre was a lieutenant now, and fought with the patriot armies in the first Battle of Carabobo and again at La Puerta, when Bolívar's forces were overwhelmed by the brutal Boves and his men. It takes a look at a family like that of Antonio Sucre to make us realize what this South American revolution meant in human suffering to the colonists. His father and uncle were in the war. In the reign of terror which Boves and his *llanero* hordes created in Venezuela, four members of his family were

killed, two brothers shot as prisoners of war, a third assassinated while ill in a hospital, and a sister actually
frightened to death during one of Boves' raids. The
young lieutenant who went once more into exile was a
man consecrated to the cause of freedom by personal suffering and sorrow.

SUCRE WITH BOLÍVAR

Young Sucre's service with General Marino in the
patriot Army of the East kept him from coming into
Bolívar's service until 1820. His talents were then recognized by the Liberator, who found him brave, honest and
capable, as well as free from self-seeking. His first important commission was an errand to the West Indies, to
buy guns, lead, sabres, and uniforms with eighty thousand
pesos which Bolívar entrusted to him. This mission he fulfilled promptly and successfully. It was at about this time
that Bolívar made his prophetic utterance about Sucre.
"Strange as it may seem," he said, "his ability is not known
or even suspected. I am decided to make him known, and
am convinced that some day he will compete with me."

For seven years now the war had been carried on with
cruelty on both sides. When Bolívar came over the mountains from New Granada, he gave to his officers the order
of "War to the Death" which was his answer to the cruelty
of the Spaniards. From that time on the contest had been
carried on in that spirit. Now General Morillo was in
command of the Spanish forces, a veteran soldier from the
battlefields of Europe who had a knowledge of the cus-

toms of more civilized warfare. In this year of 1820 there came from Morillo the proposal for an armistice, a proposal forced on him by the orders of King Ferdinand. Part of the triumph for Bolívar in this request was that he was now recognized as a belligerent, not as a guerrilla chieftain or a rebel or a bandit. The war had come nearer to the level of a combat between equals.

Sucre was one of Bolívar's delegates sent to meet Morillo's representatives and fix conditions for the armistice, with the stated purpose, too, of "regularizing the war." The delegates met at Trujillo and signed there a convention, on November 25, 1820, which has been recognized ever since as the first American document establishing international law. It dealt with humane treatment of prisoners, exchange of prisoners, conditions of armistice, and other points which have since been agreed upon as the basic rules of fair warfare. The treaty was drafted by General Sucre, who offered it to the Spanish commander. Bolívar recognized its source when he said: "This treaty is worthy of General Sucre's soul. . . . It will be eternal as a most beautiful emblem of mercy applied to war."

SUCRE FREES QUITO (ECUADOR)

Sucre's next task was a military one of unusual importance and difficulty for a young man then only twenty-five years old. Over on the Pacific coast, south of New Granada (now Colombia) and north of Peru, lay the presidency of Quito, still under Spanish rule. Here Pizarro had made his first landing, at this northern outpost of the Inca empire. Here in 1809 the first South American movement for freedom from Spain had begun when a group of creoles decided to overthrow Castilla, the Spanish president, and create a governing *junta* of their own. On the night of August 9th they met in the house of a patriot lady whose name has been held in honor these hundred and more years, Dona Manuela Canizaries, and planned the moves of the next day. The plan succeeded for the time, but within the year Castilla regained control and followed his victory by frightful massacres. For six years the inhabitants appeared submissive, but in 1820 the people of the port city of Guayaquil, thirty miles up the broad river from the coast, rebelled again, encouraged by San Martín's successes in Peru and Bolívar's onward march into Colombia. Again the royalists won control, but it was an uncertain victory over a restless and dissatisfied province.

Bolívar was determined to free Quito and join it with New Granada in his great northern state of Colombia. To this end he dispatched his ablest general, Sucre, to bring it rescue by sea, while he himself would come down from the north and meet him on land. Bolívar meanwhile was crossing to Venezuela, where he won on June 24, 1821, the decisive battle of Carabobo, insuring Venezuelan independence.

Sucre's task was not easy. In April, 1821, he and his soldiers sailed southward from Colombia. The promise had been of one thousand men, but Sucre afterward claimed that he did not have so many. He had to move

ON THE SLOPES OF PICHINCHA, ECUADOR

slowly, for the men were in poor condition. That spring he signed an agreement with the revolutionary *junta* at Guayaquil, by which these patriots placed themselves under Bolívar's protection. Sucre was a wise general. He had sent north to Colombia for reënforcements, and did not wish to move until they came. But his fellow officers pressed him, and he finally fought engagements with the royalists, but won no decisive victory. It was a huge undertaking to gather patriot recruits from the country, train them, muster supplies, and carry on his campaign in an unknown mountain region which was wholly different from the plains of Venezuela and the river valley of the Orinoco, with which he was familiar. As one Spanish historian has said, "This was a struggle against ravines and cliffs, torrents and precipices, rather than against men."

At last he came to the neighborhood of the city of Quito, the Spanish stronghold. He had gained a position on the heights of Pichincha, the great volcano, which overlooked the city. The Spaniards were forced to give battle against him in this spot which gave to him the advantage, or else to wait and allow Bolívar, who was fast moving south, to meet him. They chose to fight, and on a memorable day, May 24, 1822, Sucre won the Battle of Pichincha, defeating decisively the Spanish forces. The following day he entered the city of Quito as victor, to the plaudits of the rejoicing citizens. Three hundred years to the month after Pizarro had brought Spanish rule to Quito, Sucre had received surrender from the Spaniards.

Bolívar arrived within a month, and the province was joined to the Colombian republic. That summer came his meeting with San Martín in Guayaquil, and Bolívar's decision to go over and free Peru. Meanwhile in Quito young General Sucre had met his future wife, Dona Maria Carcelen.

There are those who call Sucre the "father of Ecuador," because of this triumph at Pichincha. Yet the independent republic of Ecuador did not begin for a few more years, until the Bolívar union of the three states fell apart and each region asserted its separate nationality. But Sucre did give freedom to the country. He was its liberator, as the statue in the plaza of the city of Quito indicates. There he stands to this day, high above the people, with his right hand pointing towards the mountain battlefield where freedom was won.

ON TO AYACUCHO

From this time on General Sucre was, as O'Leary has said, "the right arm of the Liberator and the principal support of the army." Bolívar's secretary gives us a clear picture of the young man, now only in his twenty-eighth year. "Active, methodical, punctual, indefatigable," he calls him, and tells how he crossed the dreaded Andes three times and explored places in the Cordilleras which had never before been visited. But what impressed most those who looked on, was the young man's spirit of self-sacrifice; and they marveled, too, at Bolívar's devotion to him. "I must have with me a counselor like you," Bolívar wrote to him once, "who is able both to deliberate and execute."

It was well that there was this devotion, as of father and son, for it was to be put to a severe test. Back in Colombia the Congress, under Vice President Santander, grew impatient at Bolívar's long absence. He had chosen, they said, to become dictator of Peru and commander of the Peruvian army. How could they be expected to keep him in supreme command of their army, even if he was still President of Colombia? So they rescinded the act of 1821 by which he had been given extraordinary powers, and took away the command of the army from him, giving it instead to General Sucre. If any other man had been thus put into his place, Bolívar could not have borne it. But the relation of the two men was so close that he accepted the change without bitterness and gave to Sucre his cheerful support.

Things went badly in Peru as those months dragged on into more than a year, from 1823 to 1824. As Sucre wrote in June of 1824, "We were standing on a volcano, uncertain whether to defend the part of Peru that was left or return to Colombia." But the two men were determined to drive the Spanish forces out of the country. The story of the campaign is too long to tell here. But at last there came the time when Sucre, who was then in supreme command, decided to offer battle as soon as possible, even though his forces were not the equal of those of the Spanish viceroy.

On December 9, 1824, the two armies met at the plain of

Ayacucho, the so-called "corner of death" which had been an ancient Inca battlefield. Sucre and his men had seemed to be caught in a trap. The ravine had seemed impassable. But during the night of December 5th they had crossed the precipice in silence; the next day they had pretended to retreat, and now the battle line was drawn. General Sucre rode along its length with a special word for each battalion.

To the Peruvians he said, "Conquer today, and you will have given freedom to your country and to America."

To the men of the plains, "Long live the unconquered plainsmen."

Each company had its word, and then to all he said: "Soldiers, the fate of South America depends upon today's efforts."

One other word beside the General's is remembered from that day. To Sucre's fellow-officer, young José Cordoba, had been given the duty of destroying the royalist division at the bottom of the ravine. As the company started down, the twenty-four-year-old leader killed his horse, saying that so he would have no chance to retreat. His men asked him for instructions as to the method of march. With what step they should advance? Cordoba spoke then his immortal words: "What step? Step to conquer." No schoolboy in all South America would ever fail to know those words and the story back of them.

This was no conflict of untrained men. Both armies were superb fighters. The engagement proceeded on military lines. An Englishman serving with Sucre said that it was the most brilliant battle ever fought in South America. "It was not," he declared, "a victory of mere chance, but the result of the most determined bravery and an irresistible onset conceived and executed at the proper moment." The hours went on towards patriot victory which came in the late afternoon. The viceroy had been wounded; his army was defeated. He appeared before General Sucre's tent to surrender his sword and admit defeat, and the General took him inside. Soon all the officers followed him, and were received most courteously by Sucre, who shared what food he had with them and drafted the terms of surrender.

The spirit which had shown itself in the armistice agreement with General Morillo appeared again here. General Sucre said that he felt it to be worthy of American generosity to concede some honors to vanquished soldiers who had been victorious in Peru for fourteen years. Spanish generals and officers could return to Spain with their transportation expenses paid by Peru, but if any of them wished to stay, there was to be no discrimination against them. They would be considered Peruvians. Prisoners were to be freed, and generals and officers were to keep their uniforms and swords. It was a generous gesture to a defeated army, the last Spanish army in South America.

On Christmas day, Bolívar, who had received word of the victory, issued his message of congratulation to the victorious army. "The battle of Ayacucho is the summit of American glory," he said, "and it is the work of General Sucre. The preparation has been perfect and the execution almost superhuman. . . . Just as Waterloo decided the destiny of Europe, so Ayacucho has decided the destiny of American nations. . . . General Sucre is the hero of Ayacucho; he is the redeemer of the Children of the Sun. He has broken the chains with which Pizarro bound the empire of the Incas."

Sucre replied modestly that equal honors were due to Bolívar, "the genius of America who gave me an army which he himself had organized." That was his public utterance, and to Bolívar, in response to his public offer of the title of "General Liberator of Peru," he wrote a personal note saying that the title should be returned to the man who deserved it. "I have enough," he said, "with a little corner in Quito and your friendship."

The best of it is that, under cover of these courteous and flowery exchanges, both men meant what they said.

THE CREATION OF BOLIVIA

There was an excellent common sense in General Sucre's dealings with people and problems, as well as a kindly courtesy. He was to enter Upper Peru, the land where General Belgrano of Argentina had held back the Spanish forces, the land where San Martín had once been in command. For thirty years before the beginning of the revolution this region had been held by the Spanish as part of the viceroyalty of La Plata, which headed up at Buenos Aires. Now there was civil war in Argentina, and the bond had been cut by the years of war. But Upper Peru had no desire to return to being part of the province which centered in Lower Peru and at Lima, as it had been in the Inca empire.

"We have to operate in a country," Sucre wrote to Bolívar, "which does not belong to Peru nor does it appear to want to belong to anybody but itself."

Wisely Sucre entered with Colombian troops only, leaving behind both Peruvian and Argentinean soldiers. But he need not have questioned the warmth of his reception. The people rejoiced to honor their deliverer.

Bolívar had the one answer to the problem. He persuaded the governments of Peru and Buenos Aires to decide what form of government they would choose. But his intention was clear. A separate state should be formed which would become one member of the great federation of South American states for which he was working— with the additional thought that he himself should be the head over them all. It was this aspiration, or the people's fear of it, which was to lead so soon to his undoing. Sucre had no such desire for dictatorship. He stated, with apparent honesty, that his most fervent desire was to retire as soon as the campaign was ended, and that in place of honors and titles the greatest reward for his services would be a passport to Guayaquil, where, as we remember, resided the lady who was to be his wife. But he saw the needs of the country and developed the plans with Bolívar.

An assembly of the five provinces of Upper Peru, called by General Sucre, met on July 5, 1825, and brought into being the new republic which was named Bolivia, with the name of its capital city, Chuquisaca, changed to Sucre.

Six weeks later Bolívar arrived, and was greeted with delirious joy by the people to whom he had given freedom and deliverance from Spanish rule.

One can but wonder what would have happened if General Sucre had been left to plan the administration of the new state according to his own ideas. Perhaps the results would have been the same. But he was left to administer instead a most elaborate constitution conceived by Bolívar and utterly unsuited to the people, most of whom were Indians who could neither read nor write, and the remainder totally unused to representative government. For such a people a three-house Congress, and Tribunes, Censors, Senators, and other officials were an impossibility. Under this form of government Sucre was nominally "elected" president, though the appointment was obviously by Bolívar.

As a military man, Sucre knew how to organize. He got a finance plan working, set up courts, built roads, put in a mail system, improved hospitals, and did what he could for education, opening primary schools in all the towns and establishing a college of arts and sciences in each of the five provinces. He revived the important mining industry, and organized schools of mines.

His strength lay, however, in the presence of his foreign Colombian army, which the people of the new Bolivia resented; and he himself was a Venezuelan. His troubles with his former officers, who sought power, and with other Peruvians, now Bolivians, began almost at once, and in 1828 he was forced to resign. Yet there seems a sincerity in the remarks made to him on the occasion of his farewell, by the President of the Bolivian Congress. "Perhaps this is the first time," he said, "that a great general, crowned with laurels, treading on the trophies of war, covered with glory and power, has respected the principles of law and led a people towards the possession of rational liberty. . . . This new country has presented itself as a living proof that it is possible to organize a social body without wading through oceans of blood." Bolivia was to have a troubled history, with a long series of dictators and much shedding of blood, but Sucre seems to have been less at fault than his successors. He was in a position where he could hardly expect to succeed as an administrator for a free people.

In the final insurrection which led to his resignation, Sucre was wounded. He returned to Quito with only a thousand pesos in his possession, and with one arm useless. During the rest of the year, the hero of Ayacucho went daily to work, riding on his mule, as he assisted in the management of his wife's farm. He had advised Bolívar to resign the presidency of Colombia before the Constitution was revised, foreseeing the trouble which came there. While still in Bolivia, Sucre had made the comment: "We Americans have all built our political houses on sand, and any daring man may overthrow them with one push." It was a prophecy which was all too true of the series of dictatorships which were to follow the freeing of peoples who were not trained in the ways of self-government.

Sucre's daughter was born in July, 1829. One hopes that

there were happy, peaceful days on the farm before he left as an elected member of the new Congress at Colombia, where he endeavored to harmonize the differences and carry out his chief's plan to keep Venezuela and Colombia united. By his suggestions at this time he made enemies of great strife and bitterness. On his way home on June 4, 1830, he was riding through a lonely forest. Those at a distance heard one shot, then three more. When they hurried along the path to see what had happened, they found Sucre dead, assassinated by enemies who had disappeared into the mountain fastnesses. He was only thirty-five years old when he died, this patriot of whom no one ever spoke a personal word of blame, this man of whom Bolívar had said, "If God should give to men the right to select the members of their own family, I should select for a son General Sucre."

SANTANDER OF COLOMBIA

*He was the "Man of Laws,"
the champion of the constitution*

ONE more figure is needed to complete the circle
of the countries and their patriot leaders in the
heroic age of the Wars of Independence. There are others
who lived at this time and did valiant service for liberty
or education, but the chief names stand out, and along
with Paez and Sucre must come Santander of Colombia.
We must be the more sure to know him because popular

history is never kind to a man who opposes a great hero. Francisco Santander was Bolívar's friend and supporter, and then became his bitter political enemy. Yet today Colombia honors them both, even as Venezuelans find a place in their roll of honor for both Miranda and Bolívar.

IN THE WARS

Francisco de Paula Santander fought for nine years in the Wars of Independence and won a high place for himself in this service. Born on April 12, 1792, he was eighteen years old and was looking towards being a lawyer, when in 1810 the revolution began in Colombia. He came of an aristocratic family, his father having held at one time the position of provincial governor. His early education was in his home city of Cúcuta, and his final training in Bogotá, capital city of the Spanish viceroyalty. His well-trained mind was a contribution which he could bring to the organizing of the patriot armies, and later to the administering of the republic.

The story goes that Bolívar and Santander met back in 1813, when Bolívar had been exiled from Venezuela after Miranda's downfall and had made his way to New Granada (now Colombia) to offer his services to the patriot cause and attempt to organize an expedition across the mountains. President Torres welcomed Bolívar, but the army officers were none too keen about this upstart Venezuelan who came into their organization and took his place so confidently. They sent him off, you remember, to a harmless-appearing place up the Magdalena river to cool his heels. Santander, then aged twenty-one, was lieutenant to Bolívar at that time, and even attempted, on one occasion, to dispute an order given him by Bolívar.

"March your division to the place where you have been told to go, or I'll shoot you," said the Venezuelan sharply; and young Santander marched.

The two men were together again at a critical moment in Bolívar's life. In 1818, after years of fighting, Santander, who was Colonel Santander now, was with Bolívar when the Liberator was on his way to join General Paez out on the *llanos*. Five squadrons of cavalry were in the neighborhood, seeking to keep the two patriot leaders apart, and a spy approached the camp of Bolívar at night, captured his servant, and learned the countersign which would pass him by the guards and the location of Bolívar's sleeping place. He returned with the news to the royalist headquarters, and a Spanish captain of dragoons took eight men, gave the signs to the patriot patrol, and got almost to the place where the Liberator was sleeping, when they were halted by the guard under Colonel Santander. Bolívar woke to hear the New Granadan challenging the arrivals, left his hammock, and retired to a safe spot in the woods where he spent the rest of the night, not returning until he was sure of safety. One more attempt on the Liberator's life had been foiled by the vigilance of a faithful officer.

They were an eager, capable, enthusiastic group, these young men who looked to Bolívar as chief. Santander was especially valuable for his ability to organize, and was

used for that service. In August of 1818, when Bolívar
was beginning to plan his march over into New Granada,
he sent Santander home to take arms and ammunition
and organize an army corps which he should later command. It was a satisfying if dangerous mission, as the
young Colonel went up the Orinoco and over into his
native province, distributing copies of a proclamation by
Bolívar stating that the sun would not complete its yearly
course before "altars would be erected to Liberty" in the
entire territory, which was restless now under the oppressive Spanish rule. The following spring Santander wrote
to Bolívar of the longing of the New Granadans for his
coming, and when Bolívar made his famous march, his
goal was the long-appointed meeting place for his and
Santander's well-trained divisions of the army. At the
Battle of Boyacá, Santander commanded the left wing of
the army, winning his part of the victory by his great
ability in handling his troops and his personal bravery.
His final commission was the pursuit of the royalists as
they retreated.

When Bolívar entered the capital city of Bogotá in
triumph, Santander was one of the two men who shared
the honor with him by being beside him in the procession
and at the official welcome. New Granada was in the
hands of the patriots now, with the viceroy retreating in
inglorious haste down the river. Bolívar established a
provisional government, leaving Santander as Vice President in charge while he went over to free Venezuela.

FRANCISCO DE PAULA SANTANDER
1792–1840
From an engraving.

AS VICE PRESIDENT FOR NEW GRANADA

There began almost at once the difference of opinion and of action which was to divide the two men in the coming years. Bolívar had proposed to the viceroy an exchange of prisoners, planning to liberate the brave Spanish general, Barreiro, and the thirty-eight officers whom the patriots had taken with him after the battle. After the Liberator's departure Santander gave an expression of loyalty, calling on the Granadans to remember always that their "regeneration in 1819 was the work of the immortal Bolívar." But at a not distant date he ordered the execution of Barreiro and all his officers. Bolívar was shocked, and reproved him severely, but Santander issued a manifesto justifying his act by declaring that the Spaniards were plotting in their prison and reminding the people of previous shootings of patriots by Barreiro and other Spaniards. Nevertheless, it was an over-severe act, however much it could be excused.

In the fall of 1819 an election was held in which Bolívar was elected President of the Republic of Colombia, which was to include New Granada, Venezuela, and, as soon as possible, the province of Quito (now Ecuador) which was still under Spanish rule. We have copies of congratulatory letters exchanged at this time between the two men, with Santander expressing his admiration for Bolívar's achievements and Bolívar commending his associate for his excellent administration of the country. A year or more later, when Bolívar was preparing to go southward with a Colombian army to free Quito and Peru, the deputies in Congress made the arrangement still more definite. Bolívar was to be in complete command of the army, while Santander, as Vice President, was to be Chief of State, managing the affairs of New Granada.

Three years later, Bolívar, who was then acting as Dictator of Peru, received word that the Congress under Santander had transferred command of the army to General Sucre. There was reason for the act, but it was a sign of the rivalry between Santander and Bolívar in New Granadan affairs. There was civil war in the great superstate which Bolívar was trying to create. Paez, head of the Venezuelan home government, had always disliked Santander and was encouraging the people to rise against him. Santander urged Bolívar to return, and the Liberator left Peru. But when he arrived, he solved the difficulties by taking over the supreme command and making himself dictator. From this time on Santander and Bolívar were openly opposed to each other, Santander declaring that the President threatened the liberty of the people, and that he would rather be under Spain than under the republic as ruled by the Liberator.

"MAN OF LAWS"

Now Santander took his stand as the "Man of Laws," abiding by the constitution and declaring for democracy in place of dictatorship at the council of ministers and congress. It was at this time that he made the speech concerning Bolívar's personal influence which is often quoted. Congress was meeting at Ocaña, and Santander bitterly opposed Bolívar's coming there because from the moment of his arrival, as he said, nobody would have any will or thought of his own. "Such is his influence and the secret force of his mind," Santander declared, "that upon an infinite number of occasions, even I, full of vengeance, have encountered him and merely seeing and hearing him, have been disarmed and have gone away filled with admiration. Nobody can oppose General Bolívar face to face; and unhappy he that attempts it." There is a curious confession here of the power of that strong personality on the legal mind of calm, deliberate, cold Santander.

Under a new authority voted by the Congress, Bolívar was again for the time in complete charge, and offered Santander, who had been thus deprived of his office of Vice President, the office of Envoy and Minister at Washington. A conspiracy to assassinate Bolívar which came to light at this time, with the Liberator's fortunate escape, prevented Santander's departure. He was suspected of complicity because of his open hostility to the Liberator, and was thrown into prison. A tribunal condemned him to death on the charge of giving "counsel and aid" to the conspirators, but Bolívar commuted his sentence to banishment. The last interchange between the two men is Santander's expression of thanks for this act of Bolívar's.

The conflict between the two men has tended to throw into the shade the good points of the New Granadan's service to his country. As Vice President he gave the new

—: 239 :—

nation an excellent start, with a good money system, improved schools, a well-trained army, and courts of justice. He did much for home industries, and his correspondence with Bolívar shows his efforts towards the creation of a company which should finance a canal or a railroad across the Isthmus of Panama. A reward for good government came to him when the joyful news was brought to the palace, where he was in charge of the affairs of state, that Great Britain had given official recognition to Colombia and the Provinces of La Plata as independent South American nations, free from any connection with Spain. It was Santander who added to Bolívar's call to a Pan-American Conference in 1826 the invitations to the United States and Great Britain to attend.

Following his banishment Santander spent three years in Europe and the United States. After Bolívar's death, when the constitution of the separate state of New Granada was put in force, he received in the United States news of his election as President of the Republic. In that office he continued the progressive measures which had distinguished his earlier administration. The years between had been turbulent, marked by much disorder. He gave much attention to education, restoring the lower schools which had been disbanded during the period of factional disputes. In the struggle for independence much aid had been given by Englishmen who were resident in the country. Now English methods of teaching and organization were adopted in the school system. Santander also gave needed support to professional schools and to the astronomical observatory in Bogotá.

But in so doing he limited the influence of the Church in educational institutions, and thereby incurred enmity. Nor was his administration free from the same harshness which had marked his earlier rule. Those who had supported Bolívar could hold no office, and others who opposed his new measures were dealt with severely. When the time came for his reëlection, he failed to hold the office of President, but became a member of Congress, where he served until his death in 1840.

Santander is remembered for his devotion to the laws of the country and to its constitution. He desired democracy and sincerely opposed dictatorship, cloaking his opposition under his insistence on a government of law and order, not force. It was an excellent platform, and he did well for his country. But he seems never to have been popular. There is mention by one of the foreign diplomats stationed at Bogotá that he did not entertain them, as was the hospitable Spanish-American custom. This man was there for a long period and went to the palace to dinner only once, while in Bolívar's time there was cordial and somewhat lavish hospitality.

A description of Santander by an English traveler in 1822 gives as good a summary of impressions of him as any which we have. He was serious, he says, and grave in demeanor, a trifle careless as to clothes, which were usually of cheap, ordinary native materials, chosen to assist the native weaving industry. Although somewhat stout, he held himself well, and his figure was graceful. His thinning hair was always well combed; his mustache was drooping, his cheeks ruddy. The eyes, according to this description, were small, gray, and lively; the nose, straight; there was a hint of a light smile on his thin, compressed lips. His friends, said this keen observer, held him in high esteem; his enemies detested but respected him.

NATIONAL HEROES OF BRAZIL

TIRADENTES, YOUNG PATRIOT MARTYR

JOSÉ BONIFACIO, FATHER OF BRAZILIAN INDEPEND-
ENCE

DOM PEDRO I, A SOUTH AMERICAN EMPEROR

DOM PEDRO II

TIRADENTES, YOUNG PATRIOT MARTYR

"In his life is seen the influence of North American institutions on the young patriots of the South."

IN the beautiful city of Rio de Janeiro, Brazil, there is a public square named for a young Brazilian of the late eighteenth century, who was called by a nickname "Tiradentes." It was a youth movement, this early revolt for Brazilian independence from Portugal, which came before any of the similar uprisings in the Spanish-

American colonies. At the time it seemed to do little or no good, for it was quickly suppressed by the Portuguese authorities. Yet the memory of it has lasted all these years, because of the valor and self-sacrifice of this young man and his companions, and because of the preparation which it gave for the successful uprising thirty years later. There are those who say that this Tiradentes was in a lesser way, like Miranda, a "forerunner of independence."

HOW THE MOVEMENT BEGAN

This youth movement started not in Brazil, where the Portuguese rulers did their best to keep from their subjects the writings of French philosophers on the "Rights of Man" and "Liberty and Equality for All," but in France, which was the home of those ideas. Brazilian young men went to Europe to get their higher education, as did the high-born youth of the Spanish colonies. A group of such students was at the University of Montpelier in France in the year 1786, three years after the close of our American Revolution and three years before the beginning of the French Revolution. They talked enthusiastically of the success of the United States in securing its independence, and longed to have Brazil follow its example and throw off the oppressive Portuguese control. Finally one of them, José Joaquim de Maia, wrote a letter to Thomas Jefferson, who was then American minister at Paris, telling of their desire and urging the support of the United States for the Brazilian patriots if the colony should undertake such a revolution. Jefferson was not unfriendly to the eager young men. He even consented to a conference with José Maia at Nîmes in southern France. But as an American official he could give no encouragement or promises, though he did agree to report the matter to John Jay, Secretary of State.

Maia died in France, and his companions on their return to their native land told of this contact of his with Jefferson and probably made more of it than they should. But they were not the only ones who were looking towards revolution and freedom. With the discovery of gold and diamonds in the captaincy of Minas Geraes, the province just north of Rio, there had come to be cities in which wealth and culture flourished. Among the intellectuals of this colonial society were poets, members of the clergy, professors, leading planters and mineowners.

Brazilians had grievances which matched and exceeded those of the other subject colonies in the Americas. Especially since the rush for gold, the region was treated by the Portuguese crown as a source of wealth, with little or no regard for the native Americans of pioneer stock whose ancestors had come out to Brazil and opened up the country. The taxes were excessive, and the government was oppressive and tyrannical. In no colony, in all probability, was there more hatred of the European rulers and their officials because of their unfair treatment than in Brazil.

Among this company of would-be revolutionists was

young Joaquim José da Silva Xavier, known to his fellows as Tiradentes, who was destined to become famous as the standard bearer for the attempted revolt.

AN ATTEMPT THAT FAILED

Tiradentes was a lieutenant of militia who went up and down the captaincy on his official duties, and journeyed also southward to Rio de Janeiro. He was an ardent republican, a young man of high family and of good education who was devoted heart and soul to the cause of freedom. Wherever he went he carried with him a copy of the Constitution of the United States which he read to anyone whom he could interest, telling meanwhile of the glories of an independent Brazil. His enthusiasm led him beyond the limits of prudence. Indeed, he seems to have been far more rash in his talk than a wiser, older man would have been or than many of his comrades were. But for this free talk he was to pay dearly.

The government took this moment in the year 1789 to announce its intention to collect back taxes. Many of these dues on mining and other properties had been allowed to run along if their owners could not pay them, until now they amounted to large sums of money. This action roused the patriots to fresh indignation. Now surely, they thought, was the time to strike, counting on popular support from the angry people.

It is interesting to notice that this uprising is never spoken of by Brazilian historians as a revolution. It is a conspiracy, known as the "Inconfidencia," which may be translated literally by the words, "lack of confidence." The people had lost confidence in their government.

News of the plot could not fail to come to the ears of the Portuguese authorities. The wonder was that they did not hear of it sooner, for the plan was widely known. At the last, some of its pretended friends betrayed its secrets, hoping thus to save themselves from paying their own heavy taxes. The conspirators were promptly seized and thrown into prison; and among them was their leader, Claudio Manuel da Costa, and Xavier, known as Tiradentes.

Their capture might easily have ended the matter, and doubtless the Portuguese officials expected that it would. But these young men were from the first families of their captaincies of Minas Geraes and São Paulo, and had powerful friends. Moreover, there were numbers of people who sympathized deeply with their cause. They were kept in prison during a trial which lasted, off and on, for nearly two years. The immediate purpose of their revolt was achieved. The high back taxes were promptly revoked. But the conspiracy could not be pardoned. At the end of the long trial in the courts, most of those who were accused were sentenced to exile in Africa. Tiradentes, however, was to be executed as an example to Portuguese subjects who dared to talk or plot against the decrees of the government.

Tiradentes had shown his high character during the long months of imprisonment and in the many hours in the court room. During all this time he had been the leader of the little group. Now under sentence to die on the scaffold, he was calm and serene, saying only that he was willing and glad to give his life if that sacrifice would spare the lives of his friends and serve the cause of Brazilian independence.

The Portuguese authorities had declared that he was to die as an example and lesson to Brazilians. The manner in which he met his fate made his death not a warning but an inspiration to his fellow countrymen to work for the cause of independence which had absorbed his every thought and act.

JOSÉ BONIFACIO, FATHER OF BRAZILIAN INDEPENDENCE

"What a country it is, gentlemen, for a new civilization, a new center of learning! What a land for a great and vast Empire!"—Bonifacio, as he left Lisbon for Brazil.

IF José Bonifacio had died at the age of fifty-six or fifty-seven, he would have been remembered not as a great patriot and statesman, but as a Brazilian scientist who had won high repute among the distinguished group of scientists of his generation in Europe. Even his patriotic poems, which were written during the long period of his absence from his country, were not published until after he had returned home and taken his place as one of the leaders of his people in winning for Brazil a place as a free and sovereign nation.

He was an interesting man, as all who met him either in Brazil or Europe testify. The oldest of three Andrada brothers who all worked for freedom in their native land, he bore the name of José Bonifacio de Andrada e Silva. These brothers were the sons of a Portuguese nobleman who lived in Santos, seaport of the coffee-growing state of São Paulo in southern Brazil, and a mother whose family had been among the pioneer colonists of the country. On both sides it was an ancestry of which the boys were justly proud.

SCHOLAR AND SCIENTIST

José was taught at home by his father, as was the custom of those days, until he was ready to go to school in Rio de Janeiro. At twenty he went across the ocean to the University of Coimbra in Portugal, where he graduated with degrees in both philosophy and jurisprudence six years later. But he had had another interest during his university years, which won for him an appointment that he kept for the next ten years. The Portuguese government commissioned him to go about Europe as a traveling scholar, gathering scientific material. In the course of these ten years, from 1790 to 1800, he met and became intimate with the greatest scientists of the day—Humboldt, who was to explore large portions of the South American continent, Volta, Lavoisier, and Priestley, whose names we connect with electricity, chemistry, and physics, and other men of almost equal note. On his return to Portugal in 1800 he was made Professor of Metallurgy in his own university at Coimbra, and later Professor of Chemistry in Lisbon.

There seems never to be a life connected with the patriot cause in South America which is not touched in some way by the Napoleonic wars in Europe. When Napoleon invaded Portugal in 1807 in a move which sent the royal family and court of that disturbed country across the sea to Brazil for safety, Bonifacio was called from his professor's chair to help defend Portuguese territory from the invader. He became lieutenant-colonel of an army corps formed from the students to drive back the French army. At the close of the Peninsular War he went to Lisbon where he became secretary of the Royal Academy of Sciences. In the years that followed his thoughts must have turned frequently to his native land, for its affairs had been greatly changed by the presence of the court of Portugal which was ruling its empire from South America. Delightful as his life was as a scholar in Europe, he purposed always to return to Brazil when he could. In 1816 he considered such a move, but the governing Regency at Lisbon would not permit his departure. In 1819 his opportunity came. Things were going badly in Portugal. The Revolution of 1820 was already threatening, and Bonifacio longed for his native land, feeling that he could be of service if he were there. His affection for it is shown in his farewell address to the Royal Academy of Science of Lisbon, of which he had so long been secretary, on June 19, 1819, when he was on the eve of departure.

"I have to leave for a distant land," he said, "and therefore the lessons which I have been taking from you must cease. At least I can console myself with the thought that even in the rude interior of America I shall do what I can to be useful to you. I am equally cheered by the thought that you, on your part, will fulfill the obligation which all Portugal owes to her emancipated daughter (who should now set up her own home) by sharing with her your knowledge, counsel, and instruction. What a country it is, gentlemen, for a new civilization, a new center of learning! What a land for a great and vast Empire!"

Bonifacio returned to Brazil expecting to carry on his scholarly research and devote himself to promoting education in his native land and to writing and publishing the results of his European studies. He was a man of fifty-six who might well have thought the better part of his life work to be completed. But Brazil was just stirring towards independence, in the gaining of which he was to play an important part.

BONIFACIO TAKES A BOLD STAND

In most countries, political freedom has been gained by getting rid of kings or emperors. In Brazil, freedom was helped along its way by the keeping and honoring of a

JOSÉ BONIFACIO DE ANDRADA E SILVA
1765–1838

young emperor, and Bonifacio was the man who was wise enough to see this course of action and lead his fellow-countrymen to adopt it.

It had been a curious happening which brought to this great South American colonial empire its Portuguese king just at the time when the neighboring Spanish-American colonies were fighting under Miranda, Bolívar, and San Martín to throw off the royal rule of Spain. Portugal had long depended on her ally, Great Britain, for support, and had become a weak kingdom which needed the backing of a strong power. At Napoleon's invasion in 1807 the British advisers decided that flight was the only course for the king and court, and their warships convoyed the vessels which bore the royal family with thousands of their followers in attendance across the waters to Brazil. Prince João was regent at that time, ruling for his insane mother, Queen Maria. He had been a weak monarch, but his coming gave to the South American portion of his kingdom a new importance, a new place in the world. On the advice of the English, he ended many of the aggravating trade restrictions and opened the ports to world commerce. He also did much for education, setting up a printing press and creating libraries and schools and academies for advanced study. The Bank of Brazil was founded. Bonifacio found many things changed for the better on his return to his home-land after an absence of thirty-six years.

The greatest change, and the first important step towards freedom, had come in 1815, when Brazil was

changed from being a colony to being a kingdom; one of
the three equal political divisions of the United Kingdom
of Portugal, Brazil, and Algarve (which was a province
of southern Portugal). With this, the Brazilians began
to feel independent of Europe.

In these years there was discontent on both sides of the
water with the weak royal government. In one of the
northern provinces of Brazil there was a revolt in 1817,
with a call for a republic. It was quickly suppressed, but
the word "republic" had been spoken publicly and the
memory of it remained. In Portugal a revolution took
place in 1820, with the calling of the *Cortes,* a governing
assembly which had not met for a hundred years. It took
over the powers of government, as the Spanish *juntas* had
done for that country, and prepared to adopt a constitution by which Portugal and her colonies should be governed. In Rio de Janeiro, the king was forced to swear to
support this constitution when it should be written, thus
giving the Brazilian provinces the liberal government by
the people which it seemed to promise. *Juntas* were
formed in the regions which had always been royal captaincies. The new spirit was abroad in the air, and the
South American members of the United Kingdom were
more than ready to move with it. Bonifacio was elected
vice-president of the *junta* of São Paulo, with his brother
Martin the secretary of finance.

If the Portuguese *Cortes* had moved wisely, the empire
might have been held together, with Portugal and Brazil
on equal terms within it. But the *Cortes* acted with as

much tyranny as any king could have shown. In order to keep such hold as he could on affairs, the king prepared to yield to the demand that he return to Portugal and take his place as head of the government there, with the *Cortes* as the ruling assembly. The Portuguese were jealous of the growing importance of the South American colony. They wanted either the king or his eldest son or the entire royal family to return, and poor King João, who hated to leave Brazil and disliked above everything else on earth to make any decision, had a sorry time of it, wavering between one course of action and another.

Meanwhile a strong Brazilian party was growing in power, under the leadership of Bonifacio and his brothers and other prominent men. These patriots came to advocate the return of the king to Portugal, but were desirous that his son, Dom Pedro, the crown prince, remain in Brazil as his regent.

At the end of April, 1821, the king departed, leaving his son in charge. The second step in the emancipation of Brazil had been taken. In 1815 it had been made a separate kingdom within the "United Kingdom." Now with the departure of the king, it had moved a long way towards independence from Portugal.

Again, if the *Cortes* had acted wisely, this independence might have been delayed. But as soon as they got their king back, the leaders in Portugal began to try to weaken the South American part of the empire by returning it to the state of a colony. Bonifacio had influenced the young king to stay. Now he was his chief adviser as the dispatches came in from Lisbon which finally denied the provinces the right of electing representatives to assemble in a Brazilian council and declared the country to be in a state of rebellion. The story of the young prince's part in the final move towards independence is told in the following chapter on Dom Pedro I. As we read it, we shall know that behind the scenes there was always this wise adviser, head of the cabinet or ministry chosen to carry on the government. It was he who wrote the Prince, when the last insulting dispatches came: "Sir, the die is cast, and from Portugal we can expect only servitude and horrors. May it please your Royal Highness to return as soon as possible and come to a decision." The Prince's answer was the dramatic announcement for "Independence or Death" on the banks of the Ypiranga river on September 7, 1821. The manifesto announcing this decision was written by Bonifacio, who as Minister of the Realm and of Foreign Affairs notified the nations of the world of the independence of the new empire with Dom Pedro as its head as "Perpetual Defender of Brazil," and later as "Constitutional Emperor."

Most of the Brazilian nation responded joyfully to the announcement of the new government. The remaining Portuguese troops were forced out of the country in a little over a year, partly by the valuable help of Admiral Cochrane, who had come over from the west coast of South America after his service in Chile and Peru with San Martín and now gave himself to the patriot cause here. Independence had come officially to Brazil, with little bloodshed, and the outcome was due in no small measure to the quiet leadership of José Bonifacio, who had guided the young emperor and worked to unite all the provinces under a central government.

POLITICAL DIFFICULTIES

With the departure of the Portuguese authorities, there began the period of reorganizing the great empire which extended over the whole central portion of the continent and was divided into many provinces with separate interests. The young emperor was ill-fitted for the task of leadership, and the people were as little prepared. The Andrada brothers stood for a strong central government, with considerable power in the hands of the emperor. Bonifacio showed to the assembly the troubles likely to follow on too much democracy suddenly introduced. The Spanish-American colonies had attempted that, and had been plunged into civil war, with one dictator after another seizing control. For a time he was in favor with Dom Pedro I, but as the young emperor began to show an undue amount of favor to his Portuguese counselors and supporters, the older man criticized his policies frankly and openly. "Brazil for the Brazilians" was Bonifacio's goal, and he saw too plainly that this ruler was, after all, Portuguese not only by birth but in his views. The Andrada brothers were too liberal for the king's liking in their views. José Bonifacio seems to have been unwise and dictatorial in his ways with his political opponents, and went so far as to start a newspaper in which he boldly attacked the government's policies; and by 1823 the three brothers were exiled to Europe.

For five years José Bonifacio lived in France, where he seems to have thoroughly enjoyed the unexpected leisure for one of his favorite occupations, the writing of poetry. A group of patriotic verses remains as one of his monuments. In 1828 he was allowed to return to Brazil, and it is a touching tribute to Dom Pedro's confidence in his former friend and adviser that when he was forced to abdicate as emperor and depart for Portugal, he named Bonifacio as tutor of his little son and his three daughters. The elderly statesman held the office for a while, but his enemies were jealous of his influence over the little boy who was to be emperor. In 1833 he was dismissed, and with a sign of his former hot temper resisted the removal from the position, and was arrested. His acquittal followed; the charges against him were wholly without proof. But from that time until his death on April 6, 1838, Bonifacio was closely watched by the government for such periods as he was not in actual confinement.

HIS SERVICE TO THE NATION

Brazil remembers José Bonifacio with pride and gratitude. It meant much to have a man of his brilliant mind and scholarly attainments traveling over Europe as a representative of colonial culture in the years of his study and residence abroad. Too little was then known of the Americas, and a Brazilian of his eminence reflected credit on his country. Brazil recognizes him, too, as the leading mind in the move for independence, the "brains of the revolution," which by his influence was almost bloodless. He persuaded the young prince to stay and rule, and with his brothers guided and advised him through eighteen most important months. He believed in a constitutional monarchy, and set it up; and that monarchy ruled Brazil until 1889. He saw that Brazil was burdened by slavery and began the gradual freeing of the slaves, with payment to their masters, which was continued during the century. He favored measures to civilize and train the Indians, keeping their family and tribal life. He advocated the building of good roads to hold the great empire together, and spoke strongly in favor of measures for the training of the youth of the nation by gymnastics and athletics. These were progressive measures for those days.

As a statesman he was arbitrary, and perhaps over-fond of power. Yet when he was put out of the ministry the first time, Dom Pedro was practically forced to put him back by the popular appeal against his removal. A petition came to the king with fifteen and a half pages of signatures of men of all classes of society, democratic beyond any other document of the time. The common people loved and trusted him.

One last word we of today find interesting. In 1822 Bonifacio suggested, in the presence of twenty foreign diplomats, that there should be an alliance or American free trade federation between the countries of both continents. This was before the open discussion of such a conference in the Spanish-American colonies, or the invitation to the first Panama meeting by Bolívar and Santander. In his proposals the Brazilian statesman makes us remember the words of the French Abbé de Pradt, a political writer often quoted by Antonio Carlos Andrada, his brother, "Let Europe look to Europe, and America to America, and all will be well."

DOM PEDRO I, A SOUTH AMERICAN EMPEROR

"By my blood, by my honor, by my God, I swear to bring liberty to Brazil."—Dom Pedro I.

INDEPENDENCE came to the different countries of South America in many ways, but no way was more strange than in Brazil where it was won through the active help of two emperors. The country dates its independence from two days in the year 1822, both of which center about the decision of young Pedro I, heir to the throne of Portugal, to remain in the country and so to stand for its freedom from rule by the Lisbon government. On the first date he accepted the urgent invitation of the Senate of Rio de Janeiro to remain in the country when his father, King João of Portugal, and the rest of the royal family were departing for Europe. On the second he stood by the banks of the river Ypiranga and declared for "Independence or Death" in words which have rung down the years.

HIS YOUTH

Pedro was barely twenty-four years of age when his father left him to govern as Regent in his stead, while he himself was reluctantly leaving Brazil after a fourteen-year stay. The young Prince had come to Brazil as a boy of nine, when the Portuguese court had been forced out of the homeland by Napoleon's invasion, and had led a strange life in the years between. His father had taken no pains to fit him to be ruler of his adopted country in these troubled years. Yet he rose to the call of his people in a way that has given him a secure place in their patriot annals.

It was a queer, unhappy family which came out from Portugal, and the boy could not fail to be affected by it. Pedro's grandmother, Queen Maria I, was hopelessly insane. His father, King João VI, who governed in her stead until her death in 1815 and then in his own right, was a kindly man, but with poor education and little mental

DOM PEDRO I
1798–1834
From a photograph in the Oliveira Lima Library.

ability. His mother, Dona Carlota Joaquina, daughter of Carlos IV, deposed king of Spain, was a most unpleasant person, of violent temper, given to plotting and intrigue against her husband, with whom she hardly kept up a decent appearance of unity even on public occasions. She thoroughly disliked Brazil and took no pains to hide from the people her feeling against them and their country.

Pedro, who was the oldest son, was a lively, handsome boy. Neglected by both parents and left to the care of servants, he spent most of his time in the stables of the palace. He became a fine horseman and acquired a friendly, democratic feeling towards the common people with whom he was on familiar terms. They liked the boy, but disapproved of his life, as he ran the streets and got into affairs with women before he was out of his teens. Yet he was brave and handsome and democratic, self-willed but also generous when he was not crossed. As he grew older, he was more popular than his father. It was natural that his sympathies, as he grew to manhood, should be with the liberal, Brazilian party as against the Portuguese reactionaries who were gaining favor with his father. From his youth he followed political affairs with great interest, as who could help doing in his position in these critical times?

Pedro I was fortunate in his wife, though the bad habits of his youth persisted in manhood and he was often unfaithful to her. But she allied herself with the Brazilians from the hour of her coming to their shores, and won their affection and respect as well as their gratitude for her service towards the cause of independence. Dona Maria Leopoldina was chosen in 1817 to be Pedro's wife, when he was twenty years old. In the unsettled state of the kingdom, it was thought best to choose for political reasons a princess from one of the stronger ruling families of Europe, and this daughter of Emperor Francis I of Austria was selected. She came out to Brazil to be married to the young Prince whom she had never seen. She was not beautiful, but she was well-educated and interesting, and enthusiastic over her new country from the start. In the low state to which the royal court was falling, she set high standards of culture and refinement which were important for the nation. Outdoor life appealed to her. She was a fine horsewoman, and the two young people made a pleasant picture as they rode abroad together or reviewed troops on special occasions, she in a blue dragoon uniform by Dom Pedro's side.

HE BECOMES HEAD OF THE KINGDOM

Few royal youths have come of age in as difficult a situation as did young Pedro. His father was utterly unhappy about his own position. He wanted to stay in Brazil in a life which was congenial to him. But the new governing *Cortes* which had come into power in Portugal following the revolution in 1820 wanted the whole royal family to come home. If he refused, there was danger of his losing any power which he had. Meanwhile the Brazilians were weary of the expenses of the huge court and army of followers which had come to Brazil with the king and expected to have their expenses paid by the people. The glory of having the king make Brazil his center had somewhat faded as the bills for the life of the extravagant court had to be covered by their taxes. They were moving, too, towards independence, and there was talk of setting up a republic instead of the monarchy.

At last it became evident that King João must return to Portugal at the call of the *Cortes* if he was to hold his position. England even sent a fleet to Rio to take him home, and on April 26, 1821, he was forced to depart. The scenes of the last days must have been extremely distressing to young Pedro, who was to take his place and carry on the government as regent. The queen was departing gladly and showing openly her pleasure at escaping from the land she hated. Only the oldest daughter was returning with her father and mother, the three younger girls being left with their brother in Brazil. It was a bitter thing for the king to leave the country, but he grieved even more at parting with his son.

At the end, João showed that he was wiser in his knowledge of conditions in the kingdom than he had sometimes seemed. He had watched the setting up of *juntas* in the different provinces of the realm, and knew that the Brazilians were eager for self-government. He must have known, too, that his son was far more sympathetic than he with the desire of the people for an independent Brazil. Two days before he sailed, he took his son apart and said to him: "Pedro, if Brazil becomes independent, I hope it will be under you, who will respect me, rather than under one of these adventurers."

Pedro's troubles began as soon as his father reached Portugal. The *Cortes* at Lisbon had gotten their king back on home soil where they wanted him. They could now proceed to weaken the Brazilian state of which they were so jealous. One method which they undertook was to try to keep the different provinces from acting together. Each was held responsible to the Lisbon government, instead of to any central government led by the young Prince.

The result of these efforts was just the opposite of what they intended. The Brazilians saw plainly that their country was to be reduced to the state of a colony. If Portugal had not taken this line of action, there might have been more serious divisions within the Brazilian empire. The territory was so vast that there was really little relation between the northern provinces and the southern. In the year 1821, there was a desire in some regions for republican, not royal, government. But the young Prince was popular, and had been wise in his dependence on advisers. José Bonifacio, recently returned from Europe, was his chief minister. This patriot statesman believed that Brazil was not ready for a republic. He had done much to influence the young Prince to stay, and now he threw the weight of his influence towards the setting up of a strong constitutional monarchy with Pedro at its head.

WILL PEDRO STAY?

The Prince had begun to take charge with high hopes, but the letters which he wrote to his father show that he was bitter at his treatment by the members of the Lisbon *Cortes.* They regarded him as only a boy from whom power was to be taken. He had hoped that his father could do something for him, but King João was utterly helpless. The *Cortes* had made the king practically captive, and even censored the mail which he sent to his son. As time went on, it was plain that he was weakly giving his consent to any measures they adopted and signing any paper which was brought to him to sign.

Under the influence of his advisers, Dom Pedro began to see his own position in a new light. His sympathies were all with his adopted land. He wanted to work for the freedom of Brazil, which he felt to be inevitable. If he was called home, the provinces might break apart and a troubled time result, with bitter civil strife such as was going on in some of the Spanish-American colonies. If he could stay, he might guide the kingdom safely through the change. His wife, Dona Leopoldina, was even clearer than he in the matter and was ready to help him to his decision.

As the weeks went by, the tide of patriotism rose. A strong body of patriots belonging to the powerful Masonic orders wished the Prince to remain and help them set up a strong kingdom, and the clergy, who had been deprived by the *Cortes* of their revenues, were equally with him.

On October 4, 1821, a large body of patriots took bold action, proclaiming Brazil independent and Pedro not regent but emperor; but the port cities were still in the hands of the Portuguese troops.

These were hard days for Dom Pedro. His father and the home government were ordering him to leave. His advisers were declaring that the people wanted him to stay. He insisted that he could not agree to defy the Portuguese commands until he felt sure how the two great southern provinces of Minas Geraes and São Paulo, the richest in the empire, felt in the matter. Messengers were sent hastily to these regions to get petitions urging the young Prince to stay. They returned in a surprisingly short time with petitions signed by hundreds of persons, of all ranks and all walks of life, begging him to remain. There had never been such a popular demand. The loyalty of the people could no longer be doubted.

There is a thrill in following the events of that time from day to day. In December there came to the capital city of Rio de Janeiro, copies of the decrees passed in Lisbon on September 29, suppressing the higher Brazilian courts and ordering that the Prince return at once. The young man hesitated, and even began at São Paulo his preparations for departure in obedience to his father's express command. José Bonifacio summoned his colleagues of the *junta* of São Paulo at 11 o'clock that December night in 1821, and before they parted, he had obtained the signatures of all to an address to Dom Pedro saying that his departure would be the signal for Brazil to declare its independence.

"How dare these deputies of Portugal," they said, "without waiting for those of Brazil, promulgate laws affecting the most sacred interests of each province of an entire kingdom?"

On January 9, 1822, the Senate of Rio de Janeiro, speaking for the country, made a similar appeal, which its distinguished president, José Clemente Pereira, himself took to the Prince. They did not intend complete separation from Portugal, but an appeal by a united Brazilian nation to the Portuguese government.

"Remain, Prince, amongst us," the appeal said, "to give the sovereign Congress [in Lisbon] time to become acquainted with the perilous state of affairs, . . . time to receive the humble representations of this faithful and constitutional people. . . . Give these provinces leisure to congregate round that center of union. . . . Give us time, Prince, and let us hope that the fathers of the country will yet listen to the aspirations of their children in Brazil."

The Prince received the deputation and listened to their plea. Then gravely and steadily he made his reply. He was no longer a youth, his father's son. He had become a man and was making his own decision for himself and for Brazil. "If it be for the good of all, and for the general welfare of the nation," he said, "tell the people that I will remain."

As the news of his decision spread among the people, there was great rejoicing. Now they could move forward with him at their head to the complete independence which was their desire.

"THE CRY OF YPIRANGA"

Before the year ended, the second great event took place. As soon as Dom Pedro announced his decision, the Portuguese garrison at Rio revolted, saying (very properly) that they were under orders from Portugal and must enforce the decrees of the *Cortes*. Besieged, they were forced to yield, and on February 15 they departed, meeting in mid-ocean a fleet of vessels sent to reenforce them. In late February, Dom Pedro took his oath to support the constitution, and in May he was given the title of "Perpetual Defender of Brazil." In March a squadron had come from Lisbon to take him to Spain, and he refused to go, the vessels not being allowed by the Brazilians to stay in port or land their men. He was distressed, however, over his disobedience to his father and the *Cortes*. In a letter he begged King João to understand that he was not a rebel. But he went firmly on, responding to the call of the people for the speedy calling of an independent legislative assembly which should amend the Brazilian constitution and prepare for a new and freer government.

Pedro wrote enthusiastically to the *Cortes* about that proposed assembly. It was necessary, he said, for Brazil to have its own legislature. Laws made at a distance, by individuals who were neither Brazilians nor acquainted with the wants of Brazil, could not be good. "Brazil is in her adolescence," he explained, "and is every day developing new vigor. . . . It is absurd to retain her longer in dependence on another hemisphere."

It was the cry of every American nation from North America to the tip of the southern continent which he was voicing. America must be free to govern itself and develop in its own way. When the assembly met in June, he repeated his words to them. "The great step of independence has been taken," he said. "Now you are a sovereign people. Now you have entered the great society of independent nations." But neither he nor his ministers intended to "break the ties of Portuguese brotherhood," if they could help it.

On August 14th, after the close of this meeting, Dom Pedro started on a journey through the province of São Paulo, hoping thus to strengthen its loyalty. All along his route he was met with great enthusiasm. In the capital city there was a great show of welcome, with church bells pealing and salutes by artillery. He was still in that region on the afternoon of September 7th when a messenger reached him with dispatches from Lisbon and letters from Rio de Janeiro.

To that city had come five days before the dispatches which declared Brazil to be in a state of rebellion, and ordered that members of the new assembly be tried in court. They announced, too, that fresh troops were to be sent across the ocean to quell the disorders. Princess Leopoldina presided at the Council of State at which these dispatches were read. The decision was made that Brazil must lose no time in resisting such humiliation. At the close of the meeting José Bonifacio himself handed to Paul Bregora, the booted and spurred messenger who waited outside the door ready to leap upon his horse, the account for Dom Pedro of the insulting orders from Lisbon, and of the Council's action. Along with them, according to the story, went a letter from Leopoldina to her husband containing the sentence: "The apple is ripe; harvest it now before it spoils."

The Prince was found on the banks of the Ypiranga river. He took the packet of letters and read them slowly. There was silence among the members of the small cavalcade who were escorting him, and Dom Pedro was silent for a few moments, standing deep in thought while they watched. Then he unsheathed his sword and, waving it in the air, shouted:

"The time has arrived. Independence or Death! We are separated from Portugal!"

This is what is known as *O Grito do Ypiranga,*—"The Cry of Ypiranga." From this moment Brazil dates its independence.

Tearing the Portuguese band from his hat, the Prince hurled it from him and called for an oath from all the watching company to fight for the independence of Brazil. As a Brazilian historian of the time has put it: "At Ypiranga a son of the Kings of Europe espoused the cause of American independence."

A week later Dom Pedro appeared at the theater in Rio

with a badge on his arm bearing the motto, "Independence or Death." On October 12th, his twenty-fifth birthday, he was proclaimed "Constitutional Emperor of Brazil," and signed a decree ordering all Portuguese citizens of the country who desired to adopt the Brazilian cause to wear a similar badge. On December first, he was crowned in a formal ceremony.

These were the great moments in the life of Dom Pedro I, the moments remembered with gratitude by all Brazilians. In the years that followed he was not successful in governing the newly established empire. Brazil would have been difficult for any leader to govern, and Pedro was Portuguese and could not get away from the influence of his Portuguese courtiers and advisers. For a brief time he went along with José Bonifacio as his chief minister, but later he dismissed the Constitutional Convention which he had summoned and exiled all three Andrada brothers, as we have seen in the previous chapter. The provinces to the north organized a separate "Confederation of the Equator" on the model of the United States, but were brought back into the empire after a considerable amount of fighting. The Cisplatine Province, far to the south on the edge of Argentina, which had fought under Artigas and been subdued, now revolted, and the Buenos Aires government supported it. After a long hard war this province was given independence and became the separate Republic of Uruguay.

Dom Pedro I's influence waned, and he did little to hold

his popularity. At last the crisis came and he abdicated in favor of his small son, Dom Pedro II, whose life we shall follow next. He left Brazil in 1831 and died in 1834. But the memory of him has stayed through the century. This first Emperor of Brazil did not create the separate American empire alone, nor for his own glory, but he was more than willing to side with those who were working for separation from Portugal, and by his position and willingness to lead his people he did tremendous service to the cause.

DOM PEDRO II

Known in history as "The Magnanimous"

ONE scene and one only in the life of Dom Pedro II, Emperor of Brazil for the greater part of the nineteenth century, is familiar to Americans of the United States. That is the scene which connects him with the telephone and Alexander Graham Bell.

You remember the story of the meeting of the two men. Bell had brought his newly invented telephone to the Centennial Exposition of 1876 in Philadelphia, and the judges, weary after a long, hot Sunday, were almost passing it by in their desire to get away from the building and to their evening meal. But when they had finished examining the exhibit next to it and were ready to depart, along came the Brazilian emperor with his escort. They could scarcely be rude enough to push their way out ahead of this national guest, and as they waited, Dom Pedro saw Mr. Bell and hastened to greet him with enthusiasm. Earlier in the month he had visited with great interest Bell's school in Boston and he now inquired how the deaf-mutes were, and what had brought their teacher to the Exposition. Bell explained his instrument, and the judges could not but look on while the distinguished visitor listened at the receiver which was put into his hand. "My God, it talks!" exclaimed Dom Pedro in astonishment, as the words came to him over the wire. The judges watched the amazed expression on his face, and from that hour, the telephone became one of the chief exhibits of the Exposition, and later, when the machine was on the market, the Emperor was one of the first to order a telephone for his palace in Brazil.

That United States tour which Dom Pedro made when he had been emperor for more than forty years did much to bring Brazil and our own country together. With our usual ignorance of South American life, our people were wholly unprepared to find the ruler of the great kingdom to the south a cultured gentleman, who was interested in everything we had to show; from telephones to primary schools and hospitals, from the Rocky Mountains and the

DOM PEDRO II
1825–1891
From an engraving.

Mammoth Cave to the cadets at Annapolis, and from the Boston fire department to the poets Whittier, Longfellow, and Lowell, whom he visited. Stanch republicans though they were, our people liked him thoroughly, as who could help doing? An editorial in the New York Times sums up their feeling, saying: "It must be confessed that our people do not entertain a very high respect for Kings and Emperors, as Kings and Emperors go. But a monarch so liberal, enlightened, and practical as Dom Pedro must command the respect of all sensible men."

It is hard for us of this twentieth century to remember that our neighbor country to the south was ruled by a constitutional monarch from 1831 to 1889, and better ruled than were some of the sister countries of the southern continent with their frequent civil wars and dictatorships. Brazil finally exiled this long-time emperor, but not until he was suggesting retiring in favor of his daughter. Acceptance of her would have meant another long term of royal rule, and by 1889 the country was ready to become a republic.

CHILDHOOD

Pedro was a little boy of five on that April day in 1831 when his father, Dom Pedro I bade him a last, sad farewell and abdicated in his favor. The royal child was the third boy who had been born to his parents, but the two older sons had died in babyhood. So little Pedro, who was born on December 2, 1825, was left on Brazilian soil with three sisters while only his oldest sister, Princess

Maria da Gloria, returned with the royal court to Portugal.

He was too young to remember that April day when he stood on a balcony of the palace and listened to the shouts of the people, "Long life to Dom Pedro II, Emperor of Brazil!" The people were eager to have this child, who had been born in Brazil and so seemed to be one of themselves, take the place of his Portuguese father. They were more than ready to give their affection to this "crowned orphan" for whom the departing sovereigns asked their care.

For the next three years Dom Pedro was under the care of the famous José Bonifacio, then an elderly statesman, whom the emperor had appointed as his tutor. After his dismissal because of political rivalries, his position was filled by the Marquez de Itanhaen, who loved the boy and did his best to train him for his high office. Indeed, the young emperor's training was the concern of the whole nation and especially of the General Assembly. A commission was appointed to supervise his education, and a book of full and careful "Instructions" for his teachers was published. From its pages we can get an idea of the strict and wise regime which was carried out during the next few years. The danger proved to be lest he take his studies too seriously; and a proper program of outdoor life and play had to be set up to balance his intellectual work.

Little Pedro was never allowed to forget that he was emperor. From the day of his father's departure he had to play his part in the court ceremonies, and before he was fifteen years old he had to begin to govern in good earnest.

HE TAKES THE THRONE

During Pedro's childhood the government was in the hands of a Regency. For ten years there was much disorder in Brazil. Different provinces threatened from time to time to secede, and there was constant difference of opinion as to the form of government which should be accepted. There were those who desired a federal republic, and only the provisions of the wise and liberal constitution adopted in 1824 succeeded in keeping the nation from falling apart into several warring states.

In 1840, however, things were in such a bad way that Antonio Carlos de Andrada, brother of José Bonifacio and one of the early Andrada ministry, led a movement to set aside one provision of that constitution. It required that the Regency should rule until the emperor was eighteen years old. Antonio Carlos and his associates urged that Dom Pedro II be put in full charge at once. The measure was debated for weeks in Parliament. The wisest Brazilians had been watching the civil wars in neighboring Spanish-American so-called "republics," and had been strengthened in their feeling that Brazil's chance of peace and prosperity still lay in a representative government headed by a king who was truly a king, not a child represented by a Regency. They could not wait for the young emperor to grow up, and they all knew how carefully he had been trained, and how serious and mature he appeared.

Young Pedro was not so sure of himself. He had been

watching the course of political affairs anxiously. He knew the dangers of the present system. But he dreaded to take control, for he was a modest youth, aware of his inexperience. "Can you be certain," he is reported to have asked one of his courtiers, "that with little more than fourteen years of age it is possible to possess wisdom?"

A deputation of eight delegates came to him, from the General Assembly with the plea that because of the dangerous condition of the nation, he save the throne by taking control at once. The boy received these older men with dignity and withdrew to think over their request. Shortly he returned to them and spoke the two words, *"Quero ja!"* which mean in Portuguese, "I wish it at once!" On July 23, 1840, the national assembly proclaimed him of age, and he took the oath to uphold the constitution of the land and began his independent reign.

AS EMPEROR

The story of this reign belongs in political history for which we have not the space. Dom Pedro ruled until 1889, a wise, democratic, and modest sovereign, who did well for his country both in its internal affairs and in making it a power respected by other nations.

At the age of eighteen he married a bride brought to Brazil from Europe, a princess of the house of Austria from which his mother had come, Dona Thereza, daughter of King Francis I of Naples. He was a handsome young man, six feet three or four inches tall, blue-eyed, with light golden hair and beard, and a frank, friendly expression. Both in office and as he traveled about the world in his later years, he was every inch a king, carrying himself with dignity and reserve, yet kindly as he met his ministers and subjects.

For the first few years of his reign he had to meet difficulties from the strife of political parties within his empire, but from 1850 on, his attention could be devoted chiefly to the development of its vast resources. As the years went on, railroads were built, industries were begun, education was fostered, and a free press encouraged. Immigration was welcomed, and slavery was gradually abolished. Brazil took an active part in South American affairs, intervening in Uruguay, helping in the overthrow of the dictator Rosas in Argentina, and in a long war against the tyrant Lopez in Paraguay.

The story of the revolution which drove him from Brazil is sad reading. Dom Pedro had been ill and had lost touch with political matters, both because of his ill-health and his long absences from the country, which were partly on that account. The power of the military forces in the country had grown with the series of foreign wars. With little knowledge of what was taking place among the mass of the people, these groups took over the government and requested the Emperor and his family to abdicate and leave the country. In the fall of 1889 they were forced to depart, and the two remaining years before Dom Pedro's death in 1891 were spent in sad exile in

Portugal and France. With his death the last symbol of the old regime in Brazil, and the last link with the earlier days of the winning of independence from the mother country were ended. The wonder was that the imperial form of government had lasted so long, with all the rest of the continent organized on the republican theory. That it did so continue is a high tribute to the personal popularity and wise rule of Dom Pedro II.

TWO NATION BUILDERS
UNÁNUE OF PERU
SARMIENTO OF ARGENTINA

UNÁNUE, PATRIOT STATESMAN OF PERU

*"Unánue is easily the principal political
figure of independent Peru."*—Pezet.

IN the Pan-American Union Building in Washington,
there is a Gallery of Patriots, dedicated to the national heroes of the twenty-one republics of the two Americas. For this memorial each nation has chosen the man
whom it delights especially to honor. Here the United
States has placed a bust of George Washington; and here

are portrait busts of the men selected by the South American nations, as well as by Mexico, Cuba, and the other Latin American countries.

For most of the South American republics we shall find faces and names with which we have already become familiar: Bolívar for Venezuela, where the Liberator was born and bred, San Martín for his homeland, Argentina, Sucre for Bolivia, O'Higgins for Chile, Artigas for Uruguay, Santander for Colombia, and Bonifacio for Brazil. But for Peru there is a name which is new to us, that of Hipólito Unánue, with the dates of his birth and death inscribed as 1755 and 1833. Here is a man who, like Bonifacio of Brazil, had lived a full life as a scientist and scholar before the South American struggle for independence began. Yet he was ready to contribute valuable aid in the cabinet of San Martín during his occupation of Lima, and to become Bolívar's active and helpful associate during the Liberator's period of ruling as Dictator over Peru.

It is natural that the South American republics turn back for their national heroes to the time of the Wars of Independence. But Peru does well to remind us that the leading men of that time were not all men of war. Peru was the center of Spanish culture in the New World. Her University of San Marcos had been founded in 1551, eighty-five years before Harvard College was founded in the Massachusetts colony. When Peru looks back to these days of the winning of her national independence, she finds her great leader to have been the leading figure in her university, a man who had been working for years along all lines of national betterment.

A RICH CHILDHOOD AND YOUTH

The parentage of one and another of these South American leaders is interesting, because it so often determines the career to be followed. Hipólito Unánue, who was born in Arica, a town on the southern seacoast of Peru, on August 13, 1755, was intended by his parents and relatives to be a student, and probably to take orders in the church. His father, Don Antonio Unánue, was a seafaring man from the Basque province in Spain. His mother was a Peruvian lady of excellent family, Dona Manuela Pavon. One of her near relatives, Father Osorio, was Hipólito's first teacher, and he found the boy so good a scholar that he recommended sending him away from home to study. When the boy was ten years old, he went to San Jeronimo Seminary in Arequipa, a city which lay in a beautiful valley high in the Peruvian Andes. Here he stayed until he was twenty-two years old, studying, worshiping in the stately Cathedral, making friends among his fellow students and professors, and ranging the hills in pursuit of his favorite hobby, botany. He was an active lad, full of interest in the Indian peoples who lived in the villages and on the mountainsides, and always asking them questions about their customs and listening to their stories of the far-distant past when Incas ruled the land. Later he was to write books on Indian folklore, showing how well he knew and loved his native land.

When he was twenty-two, he knew that he must make up his mind about his future, and went to Lima to consult his mother's brother, Father Pedro Pavon, who was a churchman and a scholar, soon to become professor of philosophy at the University of San Marcos. This wise man watched and questioned the boy, and came to the decision that his nephew had no deep religious calling, but was more fitted to lead the life of a scientist. He suggested that Hipólito take up the study of medicine under two noted professors who were then lecturing at the university.

PHYSICIAN AND PROFESSOR

Here in the training to be a physician the young man found his calling, as his uncle had hoped that he might, and in these years he found far more. It was the custom for a young student who wished to support himself to become either a secretary or a tutor in a wealthy family of high social rank. Unánue was fortunate in becoming tutor in the household of one of the leading ladies of Lima, the niece of the Bishop of Marseilles, and wife of a rich landowner who had been mayor of Lima in 1766. While he tutored her son and nephew, the young man was admitted to the society of one of the most distinguished and cultured groups in Lima. In her salon he met literary men and women and heard conversation such as was going on in those years in similar gatherings in the intellectual centers of Europe. It was a life into which he fitted happily and well. He became a favorite with this company of people, winning favor by his wit and personal charm as well as by his brilliant intellectual gifts. By the time he had finished his studies, he was practicing medicine as physician in this fashionable circle, and in 1789 he won appointment to the chair of anatomy in the University of San Marcos, where he had studied. In that position he began shortly to use new and original methods of instruction which brought him notice as a teacher.

We have, then, the picture of this young physician-professor, who was a scholar as well, familiar with Greek, Latin, Italian, French and English, well read in modern and ancient literature, and already writing essays on a variety of subjects of his special interest. If the life of his country and of the mother-countries of Europe had continued serene, he might have continued for many years this happy and tranquil career.

But even in days of peace Dr. Unánue was not content to stay among his books or in his classroom and social circle. He gathered in his house a group of men who called themselves the "Society of Friends of the Country." With them he delved deeper into the backgrounds of Peru and became an authority on Indian music and folk-lore. He was a friend of the Spanish viceroy, Abascal, and discussed with him the improvement of education in the country. The condition of the people interested him, and he worked for irrigation projects which should improve agriculture, and advocated better ways of getting metals out of the mines. When a medical mission came out from Europe to show the advantages of the newly discovered method of vaccination, Dr. Unánue was the first to give it his support, writing articles in favor of its adoption. Botany and physiography were his hobbies, and in 1806 there came out the first edition of his important book, *El Clima de Lima* (The Climate of Lima), which attracted the attention of scientists everywhere, among them the explorer Humboldt, who came to Peru and became one of his intimate friends. There seems to have been no progressive movement in which he was not interested, from a campaign for keeping the city streets clean to a crusade for better schools. In 1811, after years of effort, he was able to carry through the medical project nearest to his heart, the founding of the San Fernando School of Medicine.

POLITICAL LIFE

The world was changing fast in those years. Napoleon had invaded Portugal and Spain, and there was revolution in Venezuela and Buenos Aires. So important a man as Dr. Unánue could not escape a part in the political events of the time. He was sent by Peru as deputy from Arequipa to the *Cortes* of Cadiz, which had taken over the government on behalf of the imprisoned Spanish king Ferdinand, and spent a considerable time in Madrid, getting out a second edition of his book on Peru and sitting, when occasion required, in this assembly. Then he turned his face homeward, and nearly lost his life on the way, by shipwreck in the stormy passage around Cape Horn. So

Courtesy Pan-American Union

HIPÓLITO UNÁNUE
1755–1833
From collection of Luis Alayza y Paz Soldán, Lima.

great had been the danger that the University made a formal celebration of his safe return.

The advocates of independence welcomed him, too, hoping to win his support for a movement to throw off the yoke of Spanish rule. Dr. Unánue found himself in a difficult position. He had long stood for more equality of rights for the Peruvians, having written a paper which set forth in telling fashion their claims to be recognized as on a par with the Spaniards in affairs of local government. The patriots cherished this essay as one of their most precious documents. Yet he was also the friend of the viceroy, whose right-hand man he had been in working for better roads and for the establishment of schools.

For a time he steered a middle course. Like many of the South American intellectuals, Dr. Unánue favored independence and self government for the colonists, but felt that the people were not ready for democracy. He had come to believe that there could be arranged a friendly separation, with more independence for Peru, but with the government heading up in a prince of the Spanish royal family—even as the government of Brazil was shortly to be headed up by Dom Pedro.

With the coming of San Martín and his army from the south to free Peru, and with the departure of Viceroy Abascal, the picture changed.* It is to the honor of this patriot scholar that he yielded to San Martín's urgent plea for his coöperation and accepted a place on his temporary

* See page 101.

cabinet, set up under San Martín's Protectorate. Moreover, he was the only Peruvian to be on that cabinet.

As Minister of Finance and of Instruction, Dr. Unánue
was plunged into the center of the political upheaval. The
problems of the infant government would have staggered
an experienced statesman, but he managed to carry the
affairs on. His wide reading and study came to his help,
for he knew something of the theories of money and taxa-
tion from French and Spanish writers. The confidence of
the people in his integrity was of great importance. With
taxes which he was able to collect, he met the necessary
payments for salaries, reorganizing the departments of the
government to save expense. He refused to involve his
country in unnecessary debt, and did all he could to assist
in developing her mineral resources. The temptation was
to cut all expenses to their lowest level, but as Minister
of Instruction he sought an increase in the grants for
schools, fearing that war would lower the level of culture
of which the nation was so proud. It was in this connection that he made the prophetic remark so often quoted
as one of his memorials: "If the teaching of our youth is
not planned in advance, the coming generation, although
free, will be very much more limited in its outlook than
that which fought for freedom; then our sacrifices will
have been wasted." A country torn by war could have no
wiser words spoken concerning the need of protecting
and training its youth.

When San Martín withdrew from his position of "Protector" and left the country abruptly, following his inter-

view with Bolívar,* Unánue was President of the First Constituent Congress which drew up a constitution and established a republican government with a Peruvian president. When the royalists threatened the safety of the new government, he was willing to forego his previous opposition to the coming of Bolívar and to lend him his unqualified support.

Again, when peace had been restored, with Bolívar as dictator, Unánue was given the care of finance and education in the new cabinet. When Bolívar and his representatives were away on military errands, Unánue acted as Chief Executive for the republic. In these his last years, he was as progressive as in his earlier days, giving all the encouragement he could to measures for universal education. Under him the primary school system was established, the Public Library and National Museum were assisted, and secondary schools were advocated. He urged the gradual abolition of slavery, and proposed government aid for mills and factories.

Before Bolívar gave up his dictatorship and returned to Colombia, Unánue had already retired to his estate in the country. He was seventy years old, and was grown weary in his many activities. Yet in his last days he kept up his reading and writing, and regained his contentment in the beautiful surroundings of his outdoor life. To so many of the leaders in the founding of the republics there came bitterness and neglect and tragedy at the end of their lives. But Peru can be thankful that there was given to its hero

* See page 104.

the comfort of a peaceful end. He died in Lima on July 15, 1833.

On the occasion of the unveiling of the bust of Unánue in Washington in 1921, the Peruvian Ambassador to the United States, Federico Pezet, spoke words which we like to remember:

"Unánue is easily the principal political figure of independent Peru. His fame as a scientific man, the purity and austerity of his private and public life, his political experience, all combine to enhance his reputation. I consider it an honor to be called upon to withdraw the veil which still hides his marble features in this hall, pervaded by the glorious spirit of the greatest men of America. Another few moments and Unánue will again be the companion of Bolívar, of Sucre, of San Martín, and of O'Higgins. A happy destiny this, which calls him to share in effigy the comradeship of those who, in life, were his great and good friends and faithful partners in the struggle."

SARMIENTO, SCHOOLMASTER
PRESIDENT OF ARGENTINA

"The symbol of a crossed pen and sword is employed in memory of him."—Argentine historian.

ONE year after Argentina declared its independence from Spain, a boy was born in the province of San Juan, far across the continent from Buenos Aires on the eastern slope of the Andes, who was to become that republic's most distinguished citizen and its president in difficult years when its government was being rescued from control by tyrant-dictators. His story is worth our knowing not only for its own interest but because this Domingo Sarmiento was the most conspicuous leader among many in the different Spanish-American republics who stood for popular liberty during the half-century following the overthrow of Spanish control.

Independence and representative government did not come easily in South America. The people had not been prepared for it, and dictators and tyrants found it all too easy to step into the places of authority and rule their countries during turbulent years. But there were always citizens who fought against such oppression and worked for the building of a new South America, where popular education should have trained the people for self-government and peace and prosperity should prevail. Sarmiento is the man we choose to stand as the example of these patriot statesmen, for his life was picturesque and his contribution outstanding.

DOMINGO'S MOTHER

No one who visited the humble home, with its mud walls and sun-baked bricks, would have suspected any high destiny for the boy who was born there in the year 1811. Yet from the mother in that home little Domingo Sarmiento got the energy and courage which were to send him undaunted through all hardships.

Even those bricks had their story. Dona Paula Albarracine, who was to marry Don José Cleménte Sarmiento, was the daughter of an Argentine landowner who had once owned half the valley where the family lived, and worked it as a prosperous plantation, with troops of carts and mules and scores of peons laboring in its orchards and gardens. But for the last twelve years of his life he lay helpless and bedridden, and his possessions slipped away. When he died, there was little left for his fifteen children but wild land. Rich relatives were ready to help, but these were hard times and Dona Paula was an independent young woman who wished to take care of herself. Moreover, she was not afraid to work with her hands in a day when most ladies of her rank considered any kind of manual labor, except their domestic duties within the privacy of their own homes, to be so beneath them as to be almost a disgrace.

Not so Dona Paula! She wanted a home, and she knew herself to be without a dowry, such as any young woman was expected to bring in marriage. In the year when she was twenty-two years old, there was a great scarcity of woolen cloth of the kind used for the making of robes for the friars and monks. Dona Paula was skilled in weaving, as were all well-trained daughters in colonial homes, and she began at once to weave this kind of cloth for sale. She found that by diligent application she could weave twelve yards a week, though she must work all day and set up her loom at night for the next day's work in order to accomplish so much. At the end of the week she could take her work to town and get six dollars for her cloth.

In this way she got together a small sum of money, and

within a year she was ready to carry out her project of building a house on the land which was her portion of the inheritance from her father. She engaged two peons who lived on the farm of her aunts to carry on the work under her direction. The money to pay their wages must be earned by her weaving. So she set up her loom under a great fig-tree and sat in its shade all day, weaving steadily while she directed the labors of her workmen. Each Saturday she took her cloth to town for sale and brought home the money with which to pay off her two helpers.

This was the house which she, who had no father to provide her dowry, could bring as her portion when she married the young man of the Sarmiento family, who was of equal rank and station in the province but—alas!—of almost equal poverty. Here little Domingo was born. His earliest recollections were of waking to the sound of the strokes of the wheels and pedals and shuttles of the loom on which she began her work before sunrise. All day, except when she was attending to her farm and family duties, she sat under the great fig-tree whose branches shaded her from the sun and reached out over the wall of the house. Here there were orange trees and a peach tree and a little pool with three or four geese, and the small boy who played happily there never suspected the effort his mother was making to keep the family fed and clothed, while the father was off on one venture or another which might bring in money to the household but never seemed to accomplish what was expected. These were the days when San Martín was making his plans to lead an army from near-by Mendoza over into Chile. Within a few years of Domingo's birth his father was serving in the patriot army and the ladies of Mendoza were as busy weaving cloth for uniforms for the army as Dona Paula Sarmiento had been in supplying woolen for the robes of the friars.

SCHOOL DAYS

At five Domingo went to school, and here he was fortunate beyond anything that could have been expected in that remote province. These were the stirring days when all Argentina was looking towards a new age of independence, and in the minds of the leaders, education was one of the means towards that free government which they wished to achieve. Both the parents in the simple Sarmiento home were heart and soul in the revolution, and before their son could speak plainly they had taught him his letters and put him on the road to reading. They were following out the patriot decrees of the *junta* of Buenos Aires, where Moreno and Belgrano were preaching the need of education.

In 1816 the patriot government of San Juan asked Buenos Aires for teachers for the primary school which they wished to open, and a man was sent to them who was probably without equal in the country. Don Ignacio Rodriguez, whom his pupils knew as Don Ignacio, had read Scottish and English books on the new methods which were being adopted in those countries in primary

—: 301 :—

education. Four hundred children of all ages and conditions flocked to the School of La Patria of which he was made head, and with them went the little five-year-old Domingo Sarmiento, who was already able to read so well that it was the custom among the neighbors to invite him into their houses and listen with amazement while he shouted his words in a loud voice. As he was then rewarded with cakes and praise, he continued to read even more loudly, so that his uncle described him at this time as "a most troublesome and vociferous reader."

For nine years the boy went to this most democratic school, which was attended in that time by more than two thousand pupils, and in all those nine years he never missed a day. He grew weary of the school life at the last, and reports that he came to hate school. But in his reminiscences of his childhood he tells, too, of events which made a deep impression on his mind. "The sentiment of equality," he says, "was developed in our hearts by the epithet Senor, which we were obliged to give each other without regard to condition or race." In the reading school there was an elevated seat at the end of the hall, and those who earned the privilege mounted the steps to it and sat there for a time with the title of "First Citizen." Domingo never forgot the proud moment when he won this honor. Many years later, when he was "First Citizen" of Argentina as its president, he remembered how he sat as a child in that seat.

When Domingo had gone as far as he could in this San Juan school, he studied Latin with his uncle, the curate of San Juan, in whose footsteps his mother had always expected him to follow as a clergyman. He journeyed at this time to the seminary of Loreto in Cordova, intending to pursue churchly studies there, but the revolution of 1824 had sent many of the teachers away, and he returned home without entering the school. Next came study of mathematics and engineering with the engineer of the province, with whom he drew up plans for the streets of towns which were to be newly laid out. Within the same year he entered a "commercial house," or, as we should say, a store, as an apprentice. Then began the experience of self-education by reading which is most interesting to us of the United States. He was homesick for his teachers and the world of books which he had left.

"I was alone in the world," he writes, "in the midst of parcels of condiments and pieces of chintz, which I was to measure out by the yard to those who came to buy them. But there must be books, I said, which treat specially of all things and teach them to children, and if one understands what he reads, he can learn .them without the assistance of a master,—and I rushed to seek these books." In that far-away province he found such books, prepared by exiled patriots who in London had foreseen this necessity of South America to educate itself. "I read them," he says, "while I was selling herbs and sugar, and making grimaces at those who came to draw me from the newly discovered world where I wished to live. In the mornings, after sweeping the shop, I read."

From that time on he read every book which came

into his hands, and acquired a good classical knowledge. But the book which meant most to him was the "Life of Franklin." "No book," he says, "has ever done me more good. . . . I felt myself to be Franklin,—and why not? I was very poor like him, I studied like him, and following in his footsteps, I might one day come, like him, to be a *doctor ad honorem!* and to make myself a place in letters and American politics. The 'Life of Franklin' should be in every primary school. His example is so inspiring, the career he ran so glorious, that there would not be a boy at all well-inclined who would not try to be a little Franklin."

IN TROUBLE WITH THE GOVERNMENT

The next entry in Sarmiento's reminiscences comes as a shock. "At sixteen," he writes, "I was in prison." The incident which put him there was trivial, and his stay was only until his friends and relatives could come to use their influence and get him out. He had become an ensign in the militia, and was told for the third time to close his shop and do guard duty. He refused, and foolishly wrote a protest against such frequent summons, using the words "with which we are oppressed." That brought him before the Governor, and when he did not show him proper respect, he was promptly clapped into prison. Though he was there only overnight, the incident marks the beginning of his indignation against the ruling government.

His next escapade was a piece of mischief which had

no political intention. During the merrymaking at a fiesta he threw a skyrocket at the hoofs of a group of horses, and it exploded. The ruling tyrant of San Juan, Quiroga, happened to be one of the party, and the young man barely escaped another prison sentence. Quiroga was an official under Juan Manuel Rosas, who was dictator of the Argentine federation of provinces, exercising a ruthless sway and encouraging his associates in the different regions to do the same. By the time that young Sarmiento was eighteen, there was a general uprising against this harsh rule, and he left his store in charge of his aunt and joined the troops which were marching against Quiroga. For the next months he was deeply involved in the revolution, training recruits, fighting, and getting himself into trouble by his unrestrained zeal. Two hundred persons were executed as political prisoners, among them twenty of his own young friends, but by good fortune he was not among that number. Soldiering did not quench his passion for learning. While imprisoned in a house at Mendoza he saw a French library, and persuaded a French soldier to help him to master the language, translating twelve books during six weeks.

There was no safety in San Juan, and he and his family shortly emigrated across the Andes to Chile, as did many other leading citizens. There young Sarmiento's activities were varied. He had to earn his living, and he did it first by teaching a small school, then as a shopkeeper, next as a commercial clerk in Valparaiso, and finally as foreman in the mines at Copiapo. In Valparaiso he spent his half of his small wages in lessons in English with a professor from England whom he found there, and in the mines he spent all his free time reading the works of Sir Walter Scott. There were other Argentineans working in the mine, exiles like himself, and in the evenings they met and discussed politics and he taught them out of his own wide knowledge and planned with them for the future of their country.

When a chance came to return to San Juan, he and several of the other progressive young liberals did so. Sarmiento was leader of this little group in the next four years as they undertook various enterprises, the starting of a school for young women, the like of which there had never been in the republic, the forming of a dramatic society, and finally the publishing of a paper which soon got its editors into trouble because of the radical views which it expressed. Once more he must leave his home and go to Chile.

AS EDUCATOR AND TRAVELER

A liberal government was fortunately in power in Chile, with an able Minister of Education, Manuel Montt, who welcomed Sarmiento and became his fast friend. Here he became once more an editor, supporting the political fortunes of his friend's party, and being appointed by him in 1842 as the head of a normal school in Santiago, this being the first normal school in South America, and second only in date in the two Americas to the one founded in Lowell, Massachusetts, in 1839. Montt did a great educational work in Chile, founding some three hundred primary schools, which were taught by graduates of the Sarmiento school. There were few textbooks for the Argentine educator to use in his training of these teachers, but he taught them one subject and another out of his own wide learning. One of his pupils, Don José Suarez, gives a pleasant picture of the schoolmaster in these days.

> Sarmiento always treated us as friends, inspiring us with that respectful confidence which makes a superior so dear. He was always ready to favor us and to help us in our misfortunes; he often despoiled himself of his own garments to give them to his pupils, the greater part of whom were poor. He often invited us to accompany him in his afternoon walks in order to give us importance in the eyes of others and to comfort our hearts by encouragement. . . . He treated his pupils thus [introducing them to important Argentine guests] not because we were individually worthy of the honor, but to give importance to our profession, then humiliated, calumniated, and despised. But he himself, in spite of his learning and his influential relatives, was called by the disdainful epithets of *clerk* and *schoolmaster,* and was insulted to his face every day by supercilious Chileans.

This attitude to the profession of school teaching Sarmiento was able to change appreciably during his own lifetime, making it one of dignity matching, to a certain extent, that of the other learned professions.

At Montt's suggestion Sarmiento was sent by the Chilean government to study the school systems of the

United States and Europe, and his book, "Travels in Europe, Algiers, and America," contains entertaining accounts of his experiences. In Paris he met Thiers, Guizot, the historian, and Humboldt, in Spain the English labor leader, Cobden. In England he came upon the report of Horace Mann on his own educational tour of Europe, and when he came to the United States, he went to see Mr. Mann, studied the common-school system which he was then establishing in Massachusetts, and became his close friend. When he returned to Chile, he established the same system there.

From Chile he used his pen most effectively in opposition to the dictator Rosas. For years he published a periodical devoted to the interests of liberal government, with articles which so irritated the tyrant that he finally set up a counter-periodical in Mendoza to contradict what they said. Other works, scholarly, educational, and political, came from Sarmiento's pen during this period.

In 1851 he returned for a brief time to Argentina in order to give military service in the army of General Uruquiza, who was leading a revolt against Rosas. That undertaking was successful, and Sarmiento, who had won the rank of colonel, had high hopes of a better government with Rosas in exile. But he soon decided that the policies of Uruquiza were hardly better than those of the tyrant he succeeded, and withdrew his support, going into voluntary exile.

On his way back to Chile for a brief stay, he went to Rio de Janeiro, Brazil, and spent a few days with Dom

DOMINGO FAUSTINO SARMIENTO
1811–1888

Pedro II, who had read and admired his works and wished to talk with him of the future relations of Brazil and Argentina as well as of educational matters.

BACK IN ARGENTINA

Within a year the electors of Buenos Aires chose Sarmiento as their representative in the government assembly, an appointment which he did not accept. But he did return to Buenos Aires to live there as a private citizen, and took part from that time on in the affairs of the country. In 1857 he was made director of the department of schools in Buenos Aires and endeavored to start a public-school system there such as he had helped to create in Chile. It is significant of the persuasive powers of the man that an appropriation of six hundred dollars in gold which had been made was changed to a sum of $127,000, and he was enabled to set up a Model School so modern and so well equipped that a French educator, visiting it, declared that in all France there was nothing to compare with it. The supplies and apparatus were purchased in the United States.

Later, when Sarmiento became State Senator, he succeeded in carrying through a measure by which the extensive public lands which had been held by Rosas became school property. By this means there were lands and funds for the building of schools in all the provinces, which served as the beginning of Argentina's excellent school system.

As a public man, Sarmiento stood for many progressive

measures which tended to the betterment of the country. He helped to bring Buenos Aires into the Argentine Confederacy at a time when that union was still in doubt, and did much to establish freedom of speech and religious toleration by a brilliant speech opposing a state religion. For a time he served as governor of his native province of San Juan, founding a university there, and re-establishing an excellent school system. These were troubled times in the Argentine Republic, and the governor had to send out military expeditions against bandits who threatened the peace of his province, and to oppose civil outbreaks.

Sarmiento was serving as Argentine ambassador to the United States in Washington when in 1868, after a seven years' absence from his country, he was chosen its president. He had declined to go home to conduct a campaign for the office, but he was chosen by a majority so large that the election was an unusual honor and sign of confidence. Moreover, as one writer says, "his election is said to have been one of the freest and most peaceful held in the republic." The news of the people's choice met him at Montevideo on his return from the United States.

For six years he served as President, carrying on an able and energetic administration, and endeavoring to restore harmony between the provinces where there had so long been frequent strife and bloodshed, and developing the national resources. He was not without his political enemies; but when the Argentineans look back today, they are inclined to say that the peace and prosperity by means of which the modern Argentina came into being date from the term of office of the Schoolmaster President, who served also as Senator in his later days. His chief contribution was towards education. He had long believed that the ills of revolution and banditry came from ignorance. In his time the school system was greatly enlarged, and normal schools were set up, with well-trained women teachers from the United States imported to start them. His travels had given him a broad view of the world, and he improved foreign relations by inviting professors from other countries to come to the higher schools and the universities.

We of the United States like to remember his desire for closer relations between the northern and southern republics. While he was ambassador in Washington, he started a magazine called *Ambas Americas* (Both Americas) by which he hoped to establish better understanding between the two continents. Among several books which he wrote in those days was a life of Lincoln which he printed at his own expense and sent home for distribution in his own country. There was genuine mourning in the United States as well as in Argentina when there came the news of the death of the honored statesman on September 11, 1888, at the age of seventy-seven years.

AFTERWORD

WITH the life of Sarmiento, as a typical one picturing conditions during the nineteenth century following the close of the Wars of Independence, we close our group of brief biographies of national heroes. There are many men of almost equal interest and importance whose stories we should have been glad to tell. There are the men who built railroads and opened up the rich regions of the interior. There are political leaders, and writers and artists and scientists. If we began to list them, we should find the number increasing as we went from one country to another.

These men of whom we have given our incomplete sketches are, however, the leaders on whom the different republics agree as their distinguished figures. Others might well be included, but these belong without any question on the All-America Roll of Honor of the present and future. To know them better is to enrich our knowledge of these united Americas which are coming today into a new sense of their common interests as the New World of which the Liberators dreamed—independent and free so far as each nation was concerned, but with all acting together when such action would best serve their purpose.

INDEX

INDEX

INDEX

INDEX

INDEX

Uruguay, Artigas in, 121-128; wins independence, 127-128, 283

Valdivia, 92
Valencia, 146
Valparaiso, 305
Venezuela, First Republic of, 49-60, 62, 152-156; Second Republic of, 165-168; Paez, President of, 183; independence won, 200. *See also under* Miranda, Bolívar, Paez, Sucre

Viceroyalty of La Plata, 70-71, 114-115

Washington, George, 32, 131, 209-210
Washington, D.C., 28, 239, 310, 311
Wellesley, Lord Richard Colley, 46

Xavier, *see* Silva Xavier

Ypiranga, 258, 274